MW01532162

The Startup
PRODUCT
MANAGER

A GUIDE TO BECOMING A PRODUCT MANAGER AND STARTUP BUILDER

Copyright 2023 © Manan Modi

All rights reserved. No part of this book may be reproduced in any form or by any electronic or mechanical means, including information storage and retrieval systems, without written permission from the author, except for the use of brief quotations. Any use of brief quotations must refer back to the author and book.

The information provided within this book is for general informational purposes only. While we try to keep the information up to date and correct, there are no representations or warranties, expressed or implied, about the completeness, accuracy, reliability, suitability, or availability with respect to information, products, services, or related graphics contained in this book for any purpose. Any use of this information is at your own risk.

The Startup
PRODUCT
MANAGER

A GUIDE TO BECOMING A PRODUCT MANAGER AND STARTUP BUILDER

MANAN MODI

This book is dedicated to
my family, friends, and mentors.

TABLE OF CONTENTS

CHAPTER 1

INTRODUCTION

Have you ever wanted to join a startup or become a product manager? You may have wondered if you have the right background, and you might be unsure where to begin. You may be a student looking to break into product management. You may already be a product manager or working in another at a tech company, and you are looking to challenge yourself by joining a fast-paced startup. Everyone has a different journey into product management and the startup world. I want to make this book as **simple**, **straightforward**, and **comprehensive** as possible for you to become a product manager at a startup. This book will ease your worries and concerns, and it will give you the perfect roadmap to becoming a great startup product manager.

Everyone has a different story about getting into product management. I did not have the perfect background. Through trying a lot of different things and effort, I more or less found it by luck and chance. That is the story of a lot of people — they found it by chance. But with enough effort, I believe anyone **curious enough** can become a startup product manager.

The goal of this book is to help you become a product manager at a startup and learn how to continue to develop skills that will make you the best product manager you can be. Everyone is at a different stage in their process and journey, and feel free to take a look at the table of contents again to find what is most relevant for you right now.

My Background: The Journey Into Product Management

I have built products across multiple early stage startups and tech companies, helped scale startups across major fundraising rounds, helped out in hiring processes, gained exposure to a myriad of FinTech products, worked in B2B and B2C environments, understood how the venture and startup ecosystems are connected, executed and strategized alongside founders & CEOs, and more.

The companies I worked at have been backed by top investors at prominent venture capital firms. I have worked at companies that have been helped by amazing operators and advisors, such as Shreyas Doshi.

Early on in my career I joined Lendflow. Lendflow is an embedded lending platform that went through Y Combinator and has since raised a Series A. Lendflow helps small and medium businesses start lending programs, by providing them the financial services infrastructure and tools to do so. They received help from investors such as Chris Gardner, a former Paypal executive – and Salil Deshpande, who formerly was a Managing Partner at Bain Capital Ventures and a Forbes Midas list nominee. Shreyas Doshi joined Lendflow as an advisor – a few months after I joined as an early member of the product team.

After Lendflow, I joined the company I am currently at as of 2022-2023 so far. We are a mission driven startup and similarly a Series A FinTech startup.

I initially started my career in public policy and the government. After working in public policy and government, I originally joined the tech industry with the intention of helping to create an impact in the world at a grassroots level. I wanted to join tech to change the world, and I believe what makes this industry special is that anyone with the right effort and focus can do the same as well. Product Management has given me the autonomy and ability to create that change. Through my roles in product management at various FinTech startups, I have loved the opportunity to continue to build the foundation of the American economy: helping small and medium businesses, individuals, and families. I want to continue helping and scaling startups because I believe in their potential to help people.

But I started out with a non-traditional background. Anyone with curiosity can become a PM.

Let's dive into my story, and I hope it can provide one example of why and how one might get into product management.

"You can't connect the dots looking forward; you can only connect them looking backwards. So you have to trust that the dots will somehow connect in your future. You have to trust in something — your gut, destiny, life, karma, whatever" — Steve Jobs. *https://www.businessinsider.in/tech/steve-jobs-14-most-inspiring-quotes/slidelist/48046674.cms*

Growing Up — Building the Foundation

1. School. Growing up, throughout childhood, my interests academically up until high school were math, history, and English. I enjoyed the challenge of solving problems, learning about history, and writing about different topics. I wrote nonfiction and fiction for fun. For instance, in high school, I started writing about my favorite professional basketball team on a sports blog as a hobby. My articles began to get featured by Bleacher Report, CBS, and more. I enjoyed covering my favorite basketball team and athletes, and it did not feel like work. I simply enjoyed it. It was fun for me to find a community outside of school and explore my interests with a greater level of depth. These were all skills that directly built my foundation as a PM. I was not naturally great at them, but I enjoyed it. They were skills that compounded over time because I had an interest. Find the fundamental skills that you enjoyed early on: two, three, or more. These are skills that will allow you to play to your strengths.

School was great — it gave me a chance to explore multiple things and meet friends. A lot of these core skills helped me become a PM. Outside of school, that is where I had the most fun.

2. Exploring Entrepreneurship. I remember trying out basic side hustles growing up: flipping Pokémon cards, starting garage sales, running lemonade stands, launching coupon businesses on eBay, and more. It was exciting to try new things and see what worked. There was a lot of fun in selling things to people and meeting others through these activities. Through these experiences, I learned how to sell products and build small side projects that taught me the basics of business.

3. Playing games and studying how they were built. More importantly, I played video games growing up. MMORPGs and console games are not much different from traditional software products — in fact, being exposed to how these games were built over time made me gain an appreciation for the ***process of creating***. Seeing how the games were designed — the user experience and visual design gave me inspiration for what it means to build a great user journey and experience. The music and soundtracks from my favorite games will always give me everlasting memories — here and here. Games are built to resonate with people and create lasting impressions. Games utilize different senses to form a product experience.

What is now known as the "Metaverse" was a huge part of my childhood, and taught me several lessons. Games taught me how to <u>build and how to sell</u> — the two fundamentals of entrepreneurship.

4. Lessons from RuneScape and MapleStory. I loved flipping in-game items in games like <u>RuneScape</u> and MapleStory. These two games in particular have had the largest influence on me. I spent hours in the free markets, understanding what people enjoyed to buy and sell. These games taught me more about what I fundamentally enjoyed more than any other experience growing up. It taught me negotiation, psychology, economics, market dynamics, business, EQ, design, and more.

I loved trying different things, building different skill sets, and learning how to build in-game "businesses." Product management is fundamentally just that. It is about solving problems, leveling up different skills, and building things.

Being able to grow and change, through multiple **different** skills, just fueled me. The journey of making something out of nothing was what I loved.

5. YouTube and Content Creation. I used to come home after middle school and just create content for fun. It is one of the reasons I continue to create in my free time. Content creation is one of the best ways to channel your energy out into the world, find people that have similar interests, and build a community. It was about having fun and doing what I loved. It was about staying true to my interests and creating a simple experience for my community and followers.

I used to commentate over video games, review iOS apps, use video editing software, make thumbnails with Photoshop, and learn SEO. Looking back, these were PM skills. I was reviewing experiences, critiquing products, building marketing campaigns, designing screens, tracking funnels, and optimizing content.

6. Building a Newspaper Business. One of my favorite experiences was working for my high school newspaper as the business manager. Working alongside my newspaper's advisor felt like an opportunity to work with a CEO. We had to manage current clients, find new clients, manage the budget of the newspaper, fundraise through events & activities, and produce a product that thousands of people read. I enjoyed helping to build and provide a product to people. It allowed me to wear multiple hats, manage profits and losses, and lead people. I loved working to facilitate our mission of empowering student writers, artists, editors, and more. It was a very grassroots effort of running a business, as well as understanding the amount of effort it takes to market and "sell" a product to potential advertisers.

The Professional Journey Into Product Management
My Pivot Into Product Management

7. I explored several different fields in college. I did not have the most technical, design, or product background from day one. This was something I built over time. I initially pursued government and public policy because I wanted to use my career as a platform to solve problems and help people in an impactful way. Then, I thought I wanted to do finance and consulting to build up the necessary skills early on in my career. My interests were everywhere. I had to focus and choose something.

It was not until into my sophomore year that I began to believe going into tech was possible. I did not see anyone from my background at that time going into product management, as the people who went into product management usually had a series of software engineering internships beforehand. But it did not mean it was impossible. Not knowing what I wanted to do coincidentally prepared me the most for being a product manager. Going on a path of exploration gave me a diverse skill set and tools to succeed. We will talk more about this later, but I want to emphasize one lesson: your path does not have to be straightforward. You should feel inspired by knowing that *not knowing what you want to do* can be the greatest gift for you and your career. You have to start somewhere and not be afraid by the time it will take to figure it out. As long as you keep trying, you will find what fits you because you took those creative risks to explore what you truly enjoy doing.

8. I pivoted several times before landing into product management. My career journey went as follows: I worked for a local government agency, two federal government agencies, a consulting firm, a large tech company, and then transitioned to a few startups as a product manager. I accidentally found product management. I worked under a product manager at the Federal Reserve Board — I was amazed. Our team released the first iOS app in the Federal Reserve Board's history: *Money Adventure*. It felt like I was working for a startup within a government agency. This role allowed me to see what a roadmap was for the first time, work with designers and developers, and understand how to build a product. My intention was never to go into product management, but it channeled everything I loved growing up —building things from the ground up, wearing multiple hats, and solving problems to create an impact in the world.

What did I do that helped?

9. I took courses in every discipline with relation to product management that interested me. I took courses to explore product design, product management, business strategy, computer science, and more. These were some of the courses I took at my university: Digital Product Design, Human-Computer Interaction Design, Product Management, Qualitative User Research Methods, Business Strategy, Web Design & Development, Equity Investment Research and Analysis, and Designing New Ventures. You can find similar courses online, at your university, or through bootcamps. We will cover this more later.

10. It took years of on-going effort to get into product management, but I found a community. I found a community of like-minded individuals: they were builders, creatives, and entrepreneurs. I got involved in my university's app development club (Cornell AppDev) and became the Product Marketing Lead. Cornell AppDev consisted of multiple teams, with each team focusing on one app. We also had functional teams that worked on each app. We had product managers, product designers, product marketers, backend engineers, iOS engineers, and Android engineers. Being part of this community was one of my favorite memories from college. The product managers in the club inspired me to become a product manager today. I was focused on marketing, but learning the go-to-market function made me a substantially better PM today. This community inspired me to see how people were building technology to efficiently help thousands of people. I saw the vision. I knew I wanted to work at a startup full-time after joining AppDev.

I did not get to know everyone personally, but I got to see their journeys over time. They are now builders and investors that are empowering the next generation of entrepreneurs. They have created venture-backed companies that went through YC, joined Sequoia's Arc program, and were supported by great solo investors. They have become PMs and engineers at tech companies such as Robinhood and Ramp, became investors at VC firms like Greylock and NEA, designed products that continue to help millions of people, and more. Early on, through this community, I got to see what type of impact I could have in the world one day if I kept working towards my goals.

The inspiration from them was everything. Others helped me. And this is why I want to help others break into product management and startups through my journey.

11. What helped the most? I treated my own portfolio of experiences as a product I had to sell. Everyone is unique in their experiences, interests, and backgrounds. <u>You have to learn to pitch yourself</u>. The most impactful thing I did was that I explored what I was initially interested in. I was not passionate from day one. Passion was built and crafted over time. I enjoyed learning how to build and sell — the fundamentals of entrepreneurship.

Specifically, I built my skills in <u>design & coding</u>, <u>business</u>, <u>writing</u>, <u>communication</u>, <u>cold-emailing</u>, <u>evaluating startups</u>, and more. I built a <u>website</u>, wrote design case studies (<u>first</u>, <u>second</u>), <u>followed PMs and podcasts</u>, and <u>joined communities</u>. There was a lot of trial and error. There were a lot of long days and nights of experimenting different things. It was a process and journey. I want to go over what worked for me, and hopefully it can help you in your journey. Likely, you picked this book because you were interested in product management, startups, or both. I want to help you discover how you can achieve your goals through a series of practical steps I will outline for you in the upcoming chapters.

CHAPTER 2

FIVE COMPELLING REASONS TO JOIN A STARTUP NOW—AS A NEW OR ASPIRING PRODUCT MANAGER

I have spent the past few years learning from many product managers. From my own experiences helping to scale a startup team and product, I wanted to provide a few useful tools and resources that will help new and aspiring product managers. In Chapter 2, I will focus on five reasons **why** you should work at a startup.

This will be the start of my series: I want to provide the most important lessons I have learned and help you apply them. I am looking to help those who are new to product management, those who are looking to grow in their product careers, or those who are looking to break into the space.

"It's not your Y intercept, but it's your slope that's important." — Paul Buchheit, Managing Partner at Y Combinator
https://www.ycombinator.com/blog/why-you-should-or-should-not-work-at-a-startup-by-justin-kan/

The Startup Learning Curve

1. You learn to ship quickly and adapt through trial and error.

You learn to build from 0 to 1 and at scale, which is a lifelong skill that will benefit you as a product manager, founder, or any type of business owner one day. You will ship successful and unsuccessful MVPs. You will iterate on existing features until you believe they perfectly solve your customer's problem. Your work will never truly be complete, and that is the best part of the journey of being a product manager. There is always a new customer problem to solve or challenge to overcome. Your features, products, and ownership will directly impact revenue of the company. As a product manager at a startup, you affect the core strategy and learn how to think. As a product manager, you are always thinking about the **past** (evaluating features that have been released), the **present** (focusing on what you are currently executing and building on), and the **future** (identifying the next problems to solve for your customers and prioritizing them on a roadmap). Your ownership will be real, and your experiments will have a true impact.

I would recommend watching the following: *Why You Should or Should Not Work at a Startup by Justin Kan*

The Leadership Exposure of Startup Product Managers

2. One benefit of being a startup product manager is that you get to work closely with the founders and product leaders.

Especially at early stage startups, typically at Series A and prior, the founder(s) usually start out as the head of product. This may not equate to direct mentorship, but you will be engaged to learn more. They may directly delegate responsibilities to you. Your learning will be exponentially quicker, given that you will either be reporting to the founders directly (or to the VP of Product if there is one at the company). Your responsibilities will be at an all-time high, and you will need to find ways to prioritize your day to find balance and benefit your team. As a startup product manager, you learn very quickly how to interact with senior executives and deliver value to founders. Though it can be intimidating at first, you will become a stronger communicator and leader. The people skills and emotional intelligence you will develop will take you far in your career. It can be confusing to determine how to "add value" especially if you are early in your career. The value you provide as a PM comes in taking on the executional responsibilities of a founder. As you continue to develop confidence and experience as a PM, you can then influence the strategy through your history of product execution. Likely, at an early stage startup, the founders want to begin delegating product execution to a new product manager — and that is where you can come in and provide value.

A good assessment tool for evaluating a startup to join as an early PM is to first understand who you want to work for, how you can help them, and how they will help you get to where you want to be in your career. In product management, it is important who you pick as your leader and choose to work alongside. At startups, product management is a highly strategic and executional role. Ideally, you want to work for founders who inspire you. There are more factors you can consider when evaluating startups to join that we will cover in a future chapter. If you are early in your career, one of the most effective ways to become the person **you** want to be is to work for those people you look up to. And even if you aim high and they end up saying no, there is a good chance that there is someone else out there who will say yes **and** is doing what you want to do one day. Eventually, someone will say yes. In order to have them believe in you, I believe it is important to have proof or a body of work. You need to make them believe that they can take a beneficial risk on their time by hiring you. However, at the same time, you need to recognize that your time is just as valuable because you need to believe you are building and growing your career by working with them. You need to do what is best for you and your career as a product manager. One of the most effective ways to propel your own career is by working for individuals you look up to and want to learn from: _Work For People You Want To Be Like #Shorts by Gary Vaynerchuk_

It is so important to pick the right people when you join a startup as a product manager. Early on in your career, your reason to pick the right startup may be to benefit your learning and career growth. Your reasons may evolve and change as you grow. You may care more about working on challenging problems, having teamwide alignment on the product vision, finding personalities that you work well with, having the authority to work on specific types of initiatives that you care about, and more. Picking the right people and company can be challenging if you have not been a product manager or if you have not worked at a startup before. My goal is to help demystify that for you and make you feel more comfortable choosing the right startup for **you**. Later on, we will go more in depth and provide an assessment framework for evaluating startups to join as a product manager.

Startups Are Opportunity Magnets

3. Working at a venture-backed startup can be less "risky" than you think — it can, in fact, open up more opportunities.

Working at a startup that has funding can be less risky than you may anticipate at first. If you need help evaluating a startup opportunity, please feel free to reach out for advice on LinkedIn or by email. Given the level of ownership and fast career growth that happens at a startup, you will eventually become a product manager that has helped scale a startup — and your experience will continue to grow and compound over time. Product managers with startup experience will continue to be high in demand because of their ability to wear multiple hats and handle the obstacles that come with building a startup. Your tolerance for ambiguity and problem solving will increase. You will be able to handle more and more challenges in an effective way. And this is valued.

From a practical perspective, there are a limited number of experienced product managers on the job market at any given time. Most of these product managers have worked primarily in big tech. When you look at the market size of all product managers, there is a small portion of them who have worked at startups. And out of those who have worked at startups, there are some who have worked at early stage startups and those who have worked at later stage startups. There may be a few who have worked at various different company stages. The main point is that as product managers gain experience over time, their leverage increases for finding more opportunities. Getting into product management may be one of the greatest challenges, but as you continue to gain experience in product management, doors will open up for you. Founders, headhunters, and recruiters will all appreciate your ability to take on complex problems and execute on solutions for them. If you are well-equipped with a startup product manager skill set, you will be prepared to take on almost any product management role or even become a founder one day if you wish to do so. I wrote this book for individuals who may be looking for their first product management role or are new product managers. The startup product management role is one that is fulfilling and rewarding.

Also, your first role at a startup does not have to be the perfect fit. You learn with experience, so there is no need to be tough on yourself.

As you progress in product management, it can be valuable to go deep into a space and gain depth of knowledge in a particular industry or product function. The important part to remember is that you can always pivot to another product management role or startup opportunity. The depth of knowledge or industry-specific experience you gain over time is a value add for startups. As an example, if you gain a perspective on fraud detection through your time working at FinTech startups, it can be an immense value add when you join another startup that is looking to transact capital between different companies. As another example, if you build out your own YouTube channel or create your own content through a side project, that would be immensely helpful if you ever wanted to join a startup that helps creators. There are many ways you can go "deep" into a space or niche. Your goal should not be to necessarily become a subject matter expert or become the most prominent person in industry XYZ. You should pursue what you want to pursue and if you do want to specialize in an area, just be cognizant of that and that it can be helpful for your career progression in the future. It can be challenging to determine the next startup you want to join. *It can be difficult to vet startups — I would always advise doing your own research.* I am happy to talk through this one on one as well. In this book, we will review tools and strategies you can use to evaluate startups in a future chapter.

Further, if you want to become a founder one day — starting out as a product manager at a startup will teach you how to build a company. You learn how to execute on a vision and eventually define the vision over time. Being a product manager is the first step that many founders have taken. As a startup product manager, you get a front row seat to learning from a founder. You get to observe their actions, adopt their strengths, and identify how they lead. It is the perfect learning environment: you learn how to build an early stage company directly from the people who are doing it. Of course, building your own startup is more challenging. It is not the easiest transition, but it certainly prepares you for becoming a founder.

Even if you do not want to be a product manager forever, your skillset as an operator will suit you for investing as well — whether it is angel investing or being a full-time venture investor. There is less "long-term" risk in being a startup product manager because of the level of opportunity that comes with it. Enjoy the journey and focus on what is important in the present. The most important advice I would give is that you should learn how to compartmentalize: your work is your work. Time will be a key factor that makes a difference for you, so you have to let it all work out. Working at a startup is not easy. Learning comes at a cost. The role you will have as a startup product manager will not be stress-free. The most important struggle for me at times was the following question: *was it all going to be worth it?* When your friends or people you know may be taking jobs in big tech, investment banks, or consulting firms, it is going to be difficult to explain your situation. People will not "get" it. Most people have no idea what a product manager does. You might compare yourself to others and ask: *what if I went down a different path?* You have your own expectations that you may place on yourself about getting to a specific point after a certain period of time. You have social pressure of it being difficult to explain to your friends and family what you are doing as a product manager – or explaining what your startup does. The truth is, at a startup, you are going to have this pressure internally and externally. One of the reasons I am writing this book is to create a community of people if they choose to go down this path. The earlier you are in your career, taking the road less traveled is not easy. This is why having a community can be helpful. It might be hard to connect with people. If you are not in a big city with a startup community or entrepreneurs, it is going to be challenging not having people to relate to. You are going to need to make an effort to meet new people with similar interests. The later you are in your career, it is still challenging to join a startup because you have more life responsibilities. Frankly, this path you are taking is much different than other paths in that you are fundamentally learning how to build and sell a new business to society. A startup is one tangible manifestation of solving problems that have not been solved before in the world. You are constantly challenged intellectually as a product manager to think about what is next. Early on you might not have the fancy bonus check, a nice apartment in a big city, constant talking points for projects you worked on, or a big brand name to give you credibility. But what you will have built is grit. The grit of an entrepreneur will take you far. You will have to accept that you play a major role in leading a startup as a product manager. The startup will either succeed or fail as a result of your team's collective efforts. You are in an environment that breaks and builds your confidence everyday. There will be many ups and downs. You may be able to build a business on your own one day, you may be able to identify what does or does not make a startup succeed, you may be able to help other founders one day, and more. Your ability to provide value will skyrocket. You are not just another person who can be recruited out of school for a cohort. There are very specific experiences and personalities that are built through the startup journey. Your ability to maintain your sense of self as you build a startup is key. If you want to be an investor or a founder one day, I urge you to take the untraveled path. You only live once. While you have the energy, you should take that jump and believe in yourself. The most important part is to focus on the moment and build patience over time. I cannot emphasize how challenging yet fulfilling this journey is. It is not about the destination or where you go. It is about the person you become along this journey. And I will guarantee that if you join a startup, you will grow in ways that you did not expect before. My startup journey to this point is now in the form of a book, so I can help many of you in your careers. I still have not figured it all out myself, but I know that I am one step closer to it.

These are great videos that will help you learn about what it takes to embark on a journey of becoming a startup builder, and these lessons are highly transferable for your career as a startup product manager:

Chamath Palihapitiya: The Power of Slow Compounding

Source: Andrew Mason: Why Work at a Startup?

Becoming a Product Manager at a Startup

4. You do not need to start out as a Product Manager in order to become a Product Manager at a startup.

Let's say you join a startup, but you are not a PM yet. You can learn so much at a startup that would make you a better product manager — and you can start out in another role, with the eventual option of transitioning into a product manager. You can be working in customer success, sales, or marketing. In these roles, you are helping the product team in some way. You are understanding how to solve problems for customers, you are trying to sell a product or service to a potential customer, you may be working on growing the existing user base of a product, and more. It will be even more beneficial because you gain contextual knowledge to help you become an effective product manager in the future. You will find some form of interaction with the product team, and you can volunteer to help them as well. At a startup, you have a closer grasp of customers, product strategy/vision, and execution. You develop an understanding of what it takes to build, either directly as a product manager or from afar. The product team always needs help at a startup, so if you want to transition into a product role, this may be the easiest way. Google had a 20% rule that allowed its employees to explore side projects at work. This enabled employees to explore their professional interests, while focusing on their core work at the same time. If you work at a startup, you can offer to help the product team out. Startups are cross-functional by nature, so the environment facilitates teams working with one another. Resources and time are also limited for each team. You can dedicate a proportion of your time to helping or working with the product team. Even if you are busy during the day, you can help out after work hours as well. The goal would be to learn something new for yourself and show you can provide value in some way. This can open the door for you to become a product manager at the startup you are at. You can also use this learning opportunity to talk about your product experiences when looking for future roles as well. Now, when you get into a product role full-time, that is when the challenge begins.

Google's 20% rule:

https://en.wikipedia.org/wiki/Side_project_time

A great supplemental resource is this article by Lenny Rachitsky: ***How To Get Into Product Management (And Thrive)*** 🪁

Part-Time Product Management Roles

5. If you are a student or work in a different role full-time, you can always try to work at a startup part-time.

Before I worked at a startup, I worked at the Mayor's Office of NYC, the Federal Communications Commission, the Federal Reserve Board of Governors, Accenture, and Adobe. These experiences taught me a lot, but working at a startup accelerated my growth significantly. I would suggest you do anything you can to get your foot in the door and learn in a startup early on in your career.

Try to carve out time during school or after work for a startup role. It can be in the form of contract work. I learned the most about business, problem-solving, strategy, and execution after I started working at startups. Part-time roles and side projects taught me how to build, how to sell, and how to talk to customers. You can find part-time roles online and work directly for founders (more on this later). You can also find part-time work at your university in the form of student clubs, start a project by yourself, or get a few friends together to launch an idea. Even if you work part-time, you are testing hypotheses, trying different ideas, and learning from your execution.

Working at a startup part-time is a great opportunity for you to decide whether or not this career path is right for you. If you have any doubts about being a product manager, you will learn very quickly whether this is the right opportunity for you. I highly recommend working at a startup or in a product management role part-time before pursuing this full-time. Part-time startup opportunities are relatively easy to find online when you look in the right places, and you can always pitch your background in a compelling way even if you do not have explicit product management or startup experience. We will talk more about pitching yourself in a future chapter, but let's focus on where you can find part-time roles first.

To find startup opportunities, you can take advantage of the free resources available to you. Twitter is accessible to anyone. On Twitter, there are venture capital investors and product managers posting spreadsheets or creating job boards that curate startups that are hiring. Not all startups will list product roles, so they may or may not be hiring for product roles specifically...*yet.* Even if a startup does not post a product management role on its job board, you can always reach out directly to the founders or head of product at a startup. You can schedule a quick call to learn more about the startup, see if there is a potential fit with your background, and begin developing relationships with startup operators. It does not hurt to reach out directly to the founders to see if there is a need for a PM. You can always **create** opportunities.

A few resources I would highly recommend:

- The YC Startup Directory:
  www.ycombinator.com/companies
- AngelList Talent: angel.co/jobs

Do not let it stop here. Your next opportunity **does not** have to be from a startup directory or job board. This is a starting point.

Additionally, your school or program may have an email list for entrepreneurship. In my case, Cornell has an Entrepreneurship email list that has startups that are usually looking for help. Every few weeks to a month, I see people hiring for startup roles. Startups are limited in time and hiring resources, so you can always find a role if you put yourself out there. You can always put in extra effort to monitor channels for startup opportunities and reach out to founders through cold outreach. We will discuss more on this later.

You can get to know startups and founders who may excite you — and reach out to learn more. From my personal experiences, founders are very receptive. Hiring is difficult for startups. It may even be harder for a startup to hire and retain a great employee for an extended period of time, compared to you finding a startup opportunity. If you can be the matchmaker for your next opportunity and also be proactive, you can set yourself apart from the crowd and stand out. I always recommend going beyond online job posts and to directly reach out to founders. You never know where it may take you, and you may find your next startup role through a conversation. The startup journey is fun, and people are constantly looking for the next employee and partner to bring on board.

CHAPTER 3

THE FIVE SECRETS OF STARTUP PRODUCT MANAGEMENT: WHAT DOES A STARTUP PRODUCT MANAGER DO?

There are certain secrets of startup product management that I plan to reveal in this chapter. This chapter will cover the wide-reaching impact a startup product manager can have and help inspire you to pursue this path. Many product managers and aspiring product managers are thrilled by the opportunity to work at a startup, given the fast-paced environment as well as the personal and professional growth opportunities. Let's dive into more reasons why.

Why Startup Product Managers Are Builders and Product Scalers

1. Startup product managers are startup builders and product scalers.

As a startup product manager, you are solving problems and coordinating your team members towards common goals to help your business succeed. Your responsibilities will revolve around helping ship products rapidly and doing two more things: helping your customers succeed and helping your startup scale.

You need to identify the problems you want to solve, narrow down on the users you are targeting, communicate the surrounding context around the problem you are solving for to your team, prioritize the types of solutions you are forming, trust your key team members to execute, think about how to market and sell the product, and more. That is a lot. You have to do this constantly with every feature that gets built. And every time, you have to iterate on this process and think of ways to make it better.

Startup product managers are hired to execute and help define the vision that founders have. Initially, you will be picking up fundamental responsibilities of an early founder. Founders who start at the inception of a company have the very unique responsibility of also being the product visionaries and building what the company will sell. Startup product managers begin to take on more of those responsibilities. Startup product management is about building a product and thinking about how to sell the product. The level of responsibility you receive at a startup also comes with a new level of autonomy. You need to define a lot of these processes and collaborate across many teams to turn a vision into a reality.

See the following chapter for more: *"My top lessons from startup product management: the product mentality."*

What Product Management in a Startup Is Like by Instacart PM

Why Startup Product Managers
Are Early Stage Generalists

2. Startup product managers are early stage generalists with a renaissance skillset.

Startup product management is the intersection of design, user experience, psychology, engineering, business, marketing, growth, sales, and customer success. Startup product managers are operators with the perfect balance between breadth and depth. You have to learn a multitude of skills and wear multiple hats, while having a deep understanding of your product, business, and customers.

As a startup product manager, you are the startup's primary generalist. You get the chance to wear multiple hats and grow different skills in a fast-paced environment.

There are future chapters where we talk about how you can grow these tactical skills as a product manager through building businesses, working on side projects, honing your design skills, learning how to code, and more.

Startup product managers are the ones discovering and launching new initiatives, while coordinating how to execute on these projects with everyone in the company. You are thinking about the user experience (*how people will use it*), the visual design (*how it looks*), how it will be built (*how you will mobilize engineers around this problem and solution*), how it will be sold to customers and prospects (*sales*), how you will help customers use the product (*customer success*), how it will be marketed / the overall go-to-market strategy (*marketing*), how you will acquire users (*growth*), etc.

You are the central point between all of these teams. The ability to context switch and speak the language of every team will make you a multi-faceted early stage builder. Startup product managers are skilled communicators, creative thinkers, and problem-solvers. Startup product management is also the perfect crash course on learning what it takes to build a startup. Later, we will go over the steps you can take to break into product management at a startup.

How Startup Product Management Evolves by Stage

3. Startup product management changes depending on what stage you are at.

The role of startup product management can highly vary depending on the stage of the startup. A startup can go through various stages of growth. At a startup, you are likely in one of three buckets: you have product-market fit, you do not have product-market fit, or you are trying to scale past product-market fit. If you are interested in learning more about product-market fit, there will be a chapter later on that covers more about this topic. This future chapter will provide a guide that can help evaluate startups to join and go more in-depth into the qualities, factors, and signals to look for.

Let's go into detail on how your role as a startup product manager will evolve at various stages. The earlier the startup is, the more a startup product manager would be experimenting. At early stage startups, you often may not know what will work or will not work. First, you have to identify the top problems to solve and who your target customers are. Further, you may not know the exact solutions to the problems your customers have. You then have to consistently test different solutions to those problems. You will run experiments to figure out what works. You are often not sure what works or what will not work. When you do find a product that "works" and resonates with many of your customers, you will find product-market fit. You will typically know when that happens. You will know this because you will have customers who deeply want the product you are building. Customers become passionate at scale when they find something that will solve their problems.

The later the startup is, the more a startup product manager would be optimizing. At later stage startups, you are still doing experimentation — but it may not take up the entirety of your time day to day. True experimentation, through creating substantially new products, takes up a lower proportion of your time once the company has defined its core product offering. More of your time would involve optimization across the product suite. A greater proportion of your time would involve how you optimize processes or existing products. Compared to earlier stages, you will optimize more existing products and create less truly new products. There are exceptions to this at larger companies: at Facebook, for instance, they have a New Product Experimentation team where they continuously build new products and run experiments. At a startup, as it grows, you may continue to experiment on side projects. However, your core focus as a startup product manager would revolve around optimizing the main product and its feature set. It is important to remember that creating a new product is only one piece of the puzzle. Optimizing an existing product is what makes a product great. Great products solve challenging problems for customers at scale. In order to go from a few customers to many, you have to optimize the product. In that sense, the core product is changed and improved through incremental improvements. These tend to be smaller experiments. Startup teams still run large experiments at later stages. The core product would be optimized through smaller experiments, and larger experiments would be run to create new products. Most startups are limited in funding, so they have to be strategic about how they spend their time. Typically, startup product managers have to experiment more before the core product is built and will continue to experiment over time. After a startup finds product-market fit, the optimization of existing products tends to begin. For most startups, there will be a balance between experimentation and optimization as the company grows. There are exceptions to this of course. Regardless, at a startup, you will continue to work on strategic opportunities that directly impact the future of the business.

Why Startup Product Managers Work on a Startup's Most Important Projects

4. Startup product managers work on strategic projects for the business and directly impact revenue.

First, assuming that a startup is raising capital from venture investors, let's describe the inner-workings of how many startups grow over time. In order to grow, most startups have to burn money. There are startups that keep a low employee headcount and can be profitable early on. Most startups are not profitable early on, and they have to spend money in order to make money. Costs may involve marketing spend, employee compensation, and software services. Startup funds typically go towards building the product and then distributing the product to customers. Startups have a timeline for how much capital they can burn over a period of time. As a result, after a period of time, startups have to raise at a higher valuation and get to the next round as a common way to continue scaling. In order to raise at a higher valuation, they need to provide proof of their growth trajectory. The most common ways to prove growth are through revenue and customers. Startups have to grow, whether or not they are profitable yet. They have to grow primarily in the form of revenue or customers. If your revenue and users are growing, these are likely through new product initiatives that the team launched that has allowed them to capture part of the market they are operating in.

As a startup product manager, you will have the opportunity to have most of your work — strategic or executional — directly affect the startup's top line growth. You have to work on these initiatives that have a high impact because it is important for the company's survival. Startup product management is challenging: you have to make the right decisions, execute on these decisions, and keep all of your stakeholders aligned. There can be a lot of context switching and not enough time to do everything. As a result, you have to prioritize. Startup product managers have to ruthlessly prioritize in order to execute on the best ideas and opportunities for the company. In an upcoming chapter, we will go over practical strategies you can use to focus on the best ideas and opportunities as a startup product manager.

Sheryl Sandberg Wants You to Change How You Prioritize Ideas

Why Startup Product Management is Futuristic and Fun

5. Startup product management is futuristic and fun.

As a startup product manager, you will be at the forefront of innovation and building exciting products that will revolutionize a niche of the market. Startup product managers have to build the future. They have to evaluate the past and present to understand what is working for their customers, as well as what is not working. This evaluation helps inform the future. The reason why startups are hard is because you have to coordinate people around a mission and goal. You have to define the vision, help your team see the vision, and align everyone on the actions it takes to get there. Oftentimes, you are creating a solution for a problem that has not been solved effectively before. Startup product managers bring people together to manifest solutions for their customers. When you enter uncharted territory, you will have a lot of challenges — and that is where the fun is in startup product management. If you are interested in the secrets on how to become a startup product manager, we will begin to go over that in the next chapter.

CHAPTER 4

HOW TO STRATEGICALLY FIND YOUR NEXT STARTUP TO JOIN

This chapter will reveal how you can strategically find your next startup to join as a new or aspiring product manager. You can discover your next startup product manager role more efficiently through this process. Startups are a large commitment, and it is important to be thoughtful about finding your next startup to join as a product manager. Startup product management is a fulfilling journey, and you should be ready to invest time into finding your next opportunity. This chapter will simplify that process and give you a strategic framework for finding startups.

"Your work is going to fill a large part of your life, and the only way to be truly satisfied is to do what you believe is great work. And the only way to do great work is to love what you do. If you haven't found it yet, keep looking. Don't settle. As with all matters of the heart, you'll know when you find it" — Steve Jobs.
https://www.brainyquote.com/quotes/steve_jobs_416859

The Strategy To Efficiently Finding Startups to Join

1. How to Strategically Find Startups to Join:

In order to find your next startup, you need to evaluate the channels you have access to. This chapter will help demystify how you can find startups first, and next, we will go into more detail around how to create tailored outreach. I would highly recommend reviewing an upcoming chapter *"The Cold Email That Helped me Land my First Full-Time Product Manager Role"* before reaching out to a startup.

1. **Review Startup Job Boards:** Startup job boards are a gold mine for opportunities. You can look through YC's startup directory, AngelList, Crunchbase, Techstars, and other startup accelerators' websites. You can look for startups with a need for a product manager, even if they may not officially announce it. We will cover how to identify if a startup needs a product manager whether they explicitly say they do or not, and this is where a lot of opportunities can be discovered.

2. **Subscribe to Newsletters:** There are several newsletters that will help you find startup roles: Startup Search, Accelerated, Ali Rohde Jobs, Omna Search, Unicorner, and more. A great way to find more newsletters that have startup jobs is by going on Twitter and searching for newsletters. Through this, on a weekly basis, you will have opportunities sent to your email inbox. The average open

rates for email newsletters range around 20%. If you can make that extra effort to open these newsletters, click on a job opportunity, and apply, you will be miles ahead. If you reach out directly to the startup after finding an opportunity, that will bring your search to the next level. We will go over more on how to cold email later on.

3. **Visit VC Websites:** Venture Capital firms often have lists of their portfolio companies on their main website. Examples of firms to look into can include: Sequoia, a16z, Lightspeed, Benchmark, Accel, etc. This is not an end-to-end list of VC firms. You can Google the list of top VC firms. Further, you can segment your search by the stage or industries they focus on. These VC firms have websites and sections of their websites dedicated to their portfolio companies. They may have a startup job board for their portfolio companies that lists the roles that are available at those startups. Regardless of whether or not they are hiring product managers, this can be a great starting point. If a startup is funded by Sequoia, a16z, Lightspeed, Benchmark, Accel, etc, it can be a great signal of whether you want to consider joining. These are firms with strong reputations that invest in companies that they believe in. You can always reach out to startups whether or not they say they are hiring a product manager and start to build a relationship. Some startups may offer you an interview, some may say they are not hiring, and some may help refer you to another startup.

There are always opportunities to be found, and these VC firms can give you a starting point by providing you a list of their portfolio companies. However, you always have to do your own research. Just because these startups are funded by great firms, it does not mean that it is the perfect fit for you. It is a great initial signal, but you have to know what you are looking for in a startup. Choosing a product management opportunity at a startup is more complex than identifying who invested in them or what valuation they raised at. You need to **always** have your own perspective on a startup. This will also indirectly train you to be a better investor because you are "investing" your time and career into a startup you choose. We will go over later more on how to do due diligence on startups and develop an opinion for yourself on whether these opportunities are a good fit for you.

4. **Reach Out to VCs Directly:** If you know any VCs who cover an industry you are interested in, you can ask them if their portfolio companies are hiring. If you do not know a VC personally, you can still reach out. You can find conversation starters: there may be an article they wrote, a post they drafted, a startup they cover that you are passionate about, or a common interest that both of you have. You can get creative with your outreach. It is important to remember that this is a two-way street. You need to make VCs and companies they introduce you to

feel confident in your ability to succeed. The first impression is important, and you should give an authentic view of who you are. We will go over more later on how to effectively communicate and develop relationships over time. The little things are important and will help you stand out. The hard skills and experiences allow you to get your foot in the door, but the soft skills are ultimately the differentiator in helping you find your next opportunity. VCs are the matchmakers for their portfolio companies. They are always looking for the best talent and will happily help you, as you can help their startups succeed.

5. **Reach out to Founders Directly:** You can always reach out to a founder directly through a cold email. If you find the mission, the industry, or anything else interesting about the startup, you have a strong reason to reach out to a founder. You never know where cold outreach will take you. I found multiple startup product management opportunities through cold outreach. Creating a personal connection is the differentiator when finding a startup product management role. Typically, the earlier the startup is, the more closely you will work with founders as a product manager. If you reach out directly to the founders of a startup, you are starting to build trust and a relationship. You also can potentially save them time by communicating how you can be a potential fit for their startup and showing that you are interested in their vision.

Talking to founders helps both you and them understand if there is a potential working fit. If you resonate with the founders and the startup, you need to be able to pitch yourself as someone to shape an aligned vision and the execution around that vision. We will walk through the specifics on how to write a cold email to founders and follow-up steps in a future chapter.

6. **Founding Product Manager roles at Startups:** For more senior product managers or those who have worked at a startup before and are looking for their next role, you may want to consider taking on a founding product manager role at a startup. Ideally, you would have startup product management experience before taking on a founding product management role at a startup. It is not required, but it can be helpful when landing these roles. If you work for a first or second time founder, there is a chance that they are still new to product management and what the function is. If you come in with some experience building startups before or seeing how companies transform as they grow, those can be highly valuable experiences. It can also save you time and stress because you will be able to see what apply learnings across different companies. It is important to note that every company is different. Not every skill you learned before will directly translate over. The people, the challenges, and the opportunities are all

different. Please check out this Twitter post linked here for more on founding roles at startups: *https://bit.ly/3LmJgiK*

The Secret to Knowing if a Startup Needs a Product Manager

Also, how do you know if a startup needs a product manager? If there is not an explicitly posted role, you will usually know by the size of the product team. If they are an early stage startup with a small product team, the CEO is likely leading the product management function and would want to delegate responsibilities. Also, you can check if the CEO has built a company before or had experience in product management. If they have not had those experiences and if you have any form of product management experience, that is also another way you can add value. You can come in as someone that can help scale the product organization because you have done it before. Prior experience is not necessarily required to help build trust and land you a role, but it can accelerate your path to becoming a product manager at a startup.

LinkedIn is also a great tool to see whether a startup is ready to hire a product manager. Tracking increases in headcount on LinkedIn is another signal to let you know they are actively hiring, even if they do not post a product manager job. Venture capital investors often look at increasing headcounts as a signal. An increase in headcount can mean multiple things: the startup could be primed for growth, they may have the funds to hire more employees, they feel confident about hiring now, and more. You can always try to anticipate whether a startup can hire a product manager.

The founders may also put the following in their LinkedIn headline: "we're hiring!" This is the perfect signal for you to reach out and introduce yourself. Your goal is to show how you can add value in your "zone of genius" (design, business, engineering, logical thinking, clear communication, data analysis). Having a 15–30 minute call with these founders is a great way to introduce and indirectly pitch yourself. Ask what they need help with the most and see how you can uniquely provide value.

- In an upcoming chapter, I talk more about how to add value without even having any product management experience: *How to Break Into Product Management at a Startup.*

Should You Join A B2B or B2C Startup?

2. Understand the business model. Should you join a B2B or B2C Startup?

You should think critically about whether you want to be a B2B product manager or B2C product manager. B2B means business to business, and B2C means business to consumer. B2B focuses on products that are used by businesses and enterprises. B2C (Consumer) focuses on products that are used by individual people. Both have unique challenges, and it can be fun to try out product management roles at both types of companies. Evaluate your strengths first and determine what is a better fit for you. Here is a framework to use for evaluating whether to work in B2B or B2C: understand the types of companies you have worked at so far in your career, the types of customers you enjoy working with, the sales cycle you prefer, and the types of industries you enjoy working in. We will cover more on the differences between product management at B2B versus B2C companies in an upcoming chapter. You can always try both throughout your career. Careers are long, and you can always reinvent yourself to fit in either type of company. Follow where your curiosity and own growth takes you, and there is never a right answer between B2B or B2C. We will go over more factors to be aware of when picking B2B or B2C startups.

How to Design Your Own Startup Search

3. How to Create a Game Plan to Organize Your Startup Search:

You can optimize for a few factors: the type of company (B2B or B2C), vertical (industry), the role itself (PM), and stage (early stage versus later-stage). You can create a spreadsheet of industries that you are passionate about or interested in and do targeted outreach for founders in these spaces that you are interested in.

- **Type of Company:** do you want to work for a B2B or B2C company? What types of customers do you want to work with?
- **Vertical:** you can create a list of the top few industries you are passionate about (FinTech, Creator Economy, AI, Wellness, Crypto, etc). Once you make a list of these industries, you can use it as a compass for guiding you towards your next startup.
- **Role:** what responsibilities would you have as a product manager? Will your role be qualitative, data-driven, or a mix of both? Is the team operating in a waterfall or agile environment? How large is the product team currently? Who leads the product team, and who will you directly work with? Who are the key stakeholders that you will be working with? How often does the team talk to customers, and how does the team currently talk to customers — what is their process? How often will you have a chance to interface with customers? How much flexibility will you have to inspire the roadmap? How does the team think through prioritization? How do the founders and the product team work together?
- **Stage:** what stage company do you want to join? How early (pre-seed, seed, series A, series B)? What level of product-market fit are you comfortable with? Do you enjoy undefined problems that require experimentation? Do you enjoy optimizing an existing product portfolio?

See Garry Tan's video for a strong framework on how to think through your startup search:

Quit and join that risky tech startup? A guide to learning, earning & minimizing regret at startups

Secrets to Success in Your First Startup Call or Interview

4. How to Succeed in Your Initial Conversation and Interview:

When you connect with an early stage startup for an initial conversation, you may have a conversation with the founders. Your initial conversation or "interview" at an early stage startup, if you reached out via cold email, will likely be with one of the founders. If that goes well, you will be referred to another member of the team, or the head of product.

Beyond preparing for behavioral interview questions, you will need to know the product deeply. If you can understand the product, how it works, who the core customers are, and the types of problems they experience, you will be significantly more prepared for an interview. The founders or head of product are trying to understand if they can trust you to lead the future product, execute on an aligned team vision, communicate in a structured way, and identify how to improve the product. Asking good questions is the differentiator in conversations with startup teams. The ability to think critically and a track record of successful execution can set the tone. It sets the first impression — this is how you show the company that you can provide value. When interviewing for a startup product manager role, there are a few steps to success that are outlined below.

Steps to Success:

1. **Use the product beforehand:** use it, test it out, and become as familiar with the product as you can. Put yourself in the shoes of the customer. There may be testimonials from customers on the website, articles around educating their target audience, and other initiatives the startup has publicly announced that can help you understand who target customers are.

2. **Understand the context around the product:** you should look at their website, take time to analyze the competitors and market, and talk to the team. Most B2B and B2C products have sales teams that you can start a conversation with to learn more about the product. The sales team can give a demo or help you with the onboarding process. Eventually, when you do become a startup product manager, you will need to talk to your sales team. When you are building products, it is critical to understand the sales cycle and how customers are first introduced to the product. Before you go into your initial interviews with a startup, you should study everything you can about the product.

3. **Ask questions about the future of the product and show you deeply understand the vision:** given the context that you have built by studying everything you can about the product, you should be able to think through the potential long-term goals that the team may have. This will help you understand the product vision and where the product will go. The important differentiator in startup product management interviews is how well you understand the existing vision, how you can help shape it, and how you can execute on the vision successfully. This is your opportunity to be creative and analytical about the product. Product management is about solving problems and knowing what to build, as well as supporting teams to execute on a shared vision. You can show your potential when it comes to product vision by asking questions on the future of the product. Your ability to ask thorough questions will not only give you a deeper understanding of the product but also give the team confidence in your ability to succeed in this role. Doing your own research and asking questions are a good way to have your understanding of the product compound over time.

Your initial conversations with a startup are what will set you apart when you are finding startup product management opportunities. Everything from doing your own cold outreach to doing your own diligence shows that you continue to go the extra mile. It will help you also effectively vet whether an opportunity is a fit for you.

When interviewing for a new company, you need to take the time to understand the product deeply and where the future vision is headed. Coming prepared into interviews with questions is important.

- Here are a few questions you can ask to "interview" your future managers. This can help you learn about a company and make an informed decision: *https://bit.ly/3LvJy71*

If you can also anticipate the future vision and ask questions around it, you will be ahead of most interviewing for the role. Additionally, you should follow up after your interviews. Every little step you take makes a difference. Next, we will go over how you can break into product management at a startup and provide a comprehensive strategy that you can use. Regardless of your background, there is a feasible way for anyone to become a startup product manager. All you need to have is the curiosity and commitment to do what it takes to become one.

CHAPTER 5

HOW TO BREAK INTO PRODUCT MANAGEMENT AT A STARTUP

Breaking into product management is not easy, but I wanted to provide a comprehensive strategy for how you can break into product management at a startup regardless of your background. You have likely come this far because you do have an interest in joining a startup and product management. We have already covered reasons **why** you should consider joining a startup now and approaches on **how** to find the right startup to join. In future chapters, I will hone in on how to effectively do due diligence on startups and how to cold email founders to start developing relationships with startups. Now, I will focus on **two critical parts** of breaking into product management at a startup: how to pitch yourself to startups (*with or without having related product experience*) and how to construct an effective modern resume for product management.

The Simple Strategy For Pitching Yourself Successfully

1. Learn How to Pitch Yourself for a Product Management role at a Startup:

Everyone who began their career in startup product management did not have the perfect background. There is no such thing as a perfect background. This is why I believe that it is possible for anyone, with the right level of commitment and effort, to break into product management at a startup. Your current role may or may not be in product management, or you may or may not have startup experience — that is why you are here! In order to break into product management at a startup, you need to critically think about how you will pitch yourself. Before you apply to a startup or have any conversations, you will need to create a plan for how you will pitch yourself. This has to be thoughtful, and you can iterate on your plan over time. We will go over what it takes to develop an effective plan for pitching yourself as a startup product manager.

At a startup, product management is essentially a combination of different skills. You are using these different skills to help build solutions to problems. Showcasing your skills and pitching those skills well are what will help you land a startup product manager job. If you have the encompassing skills for product management (*which can also come through non-product roles*), you can break into product management. Check out the skills list further below to understand how many different skills a product manager could have — and it is not limited to these skills.

You need to show your ability to wear multiple hats. Product management is the intersection of user experience, technology, and business – but let us focus on breaking these skills down in a way that is digestible.

The Product Trifecta: Product Expertise, Product Strategy & Execution, And Product Soft Skills

Product management skills can be broken down into three categories: Product Expertise, Product Strategy & Execution, and Product Soft Skills. We will call this the Product Trifecta. A collection of skills from all three categories will prepare you to be a great startup product manager. Everyone already has some form of these skills, whether or not they have been a product manager before. The important lesson to note is that these skills can continue to be improved over time. Mastery takes time. As mentioned earlier, you do not have to have explicit product management experience in order to have used these skills before. The experiences you have had before you land your first or next product management role can be pitched to help you land your next job. Startup product managers are highly skilled generalists as we have mentioned before. In order to become one, you have to prove you have these skills and then continue to grow them over time. We will dive into the specifics of each category below:

1. **Product Expertise:** product expertise is your ability to know the product you are working on. You have to have a

deep understanding of the product and its features. It is important to identify any existing pain points as well as how customers use the product. Product expertise also involves the cross-functional understanding of how your team works with other teams such as engineering, customer success, marketing, design, etc. You do not necessarily need to be a product manager in order to be an expert of the product. In previous roles, for instance, you may have heavily used the product and been in a different role. You may have been in one of the other functional roles mentioned and worked closely with the product team before. Product expertise also involves knowing your competitors, the market you operate in, the size of the market, the niche that your product positions itself in, and any trends associated with the industry. Again, in order to have these skills, you **do not** need product management experience. You may have been a designer who analyzed competitor products, a business development employee who knew why your product was the best out there on the market, or a marketer who has targeted ads to customers in your specific niche. Another important factor in product expertise is being able to understand the qualitative and quantitative feedback on your product. Perhaps the most important part of product expertise is being able to know your customers deeply, how they feel about the user experience, identifying what your customers need, and understanding how they are using your product. In addition to this, you need to know the metrics and data for your product. You may have been a customer success manager who clearly understood how customers used your product and gathered feedback from them. Alternatively, you may have been on the growth team and tracked metrics after trying different growth hacks to improve the product experience. Product expertise is not limited to product managers. Your ability to identify and communicate how your previous experiences relate to product management will help you land a startup product manager role.

2. **Product Strategy & Execution**: you need to be able to form a product strategy as a startup product manager. This is your product vision in a communicable form: it could be in the form of a product roadmap, OKRs, and KPIs. In short, you need a plan of what you will work on for the next quarter at a minimum, set teamwide goals that you aim to hit, and identify the top problems you are solving for your customers. Strategy is important because that is how you unite stakeholders behind a shared vision to solve customer problems collaboratively. Product strategy also involves knowing how it relates to the business model and how the product will facilitate top-line growth of the company. It is vital to understand that product strategy and execution go hand in hand. You cannot have one without

the other and be successful. Strategy gives you direction, and execution helps solidify the ideas you have into a tangible product. Execution is just as important as forming strategy, if not more. Your ability to execute upon a strategy is vital as a startup product manager: whether that is running sprints, drafting user stories, writing product requirements, meeting with designers and engineers, or talking through the go-to-market strategy with your marketing and sales teams. You also need to define problem spaces and facilitate solutions: talking to customers, identifying problems to solve, prioritizing problems, creating opportunity areas for your teams, brainstorming solutions, evaluating trade-offs for solutions, and prioritizing solutions. The final bucket includes iteration – you need to continuously determine how to make things better, develop hypotheses, experiment with new features, A/B test features, and optimize the product. All of these are core skills of product management that relate to strategy and execution, which you may have developed in previous roles as well.

3. **Product Soft Skills**: the final important category of being a product manager involves how well you work with people. The people you work with will often be called your stakeholders. You may hear another term for product soft skills: stakeholder management. Being great at stakeholder engagement is key. You need to be able to

spearhead initiatives and gather people in a way that promotes innovation and inclusive decision making. Startup product managers lead across different teams and promote collaboration across functional groups. Communication, both written and spoken, is critical. Keeping stakeholders aware of initiatives you are working on is important, but you should try to involve them on initiatives as well. Product managers also need to decide what to build, and they need to be able to empower their teams. Your teams will handle the execution and get the job done. You need to guide them in the right direction and keep your teammates involved in decision making. Startup product managers need to set expectations and be clear about the goals they create for their teams, as well as inspire their team members to reach those goals. There are soft skills you may have learned in previous jobs that can translate over to startup product management. Most soft skills in startup product management are developed on the job and continue to grow over time.

Transitioning Into Product Management From a Different Role

Regardless of your prior background, you can become a product manager. It helps to be in a related role, especially if you were at a software company earlier or have some transferable skills as mentioned in the previous section. We can bust a few common myths about product management. You **do not** have to be technical, study computer science, intern in product management, work at a big tech company, or even work at a startup. These previously mentioned experiences do help, but they are not required by any means. If you are in a different role, we can talk through how you can use your experience to pivot into product management:

If you are a designer or software engineer:

- You know how to build already. You can discuss the projects you have built internally and externally, whether they are at a company or through a side project. In each of those experiences, you can talk about how you have exercised product skills. Feel free to go back to the earlier section of this chapter where we went over product skills.
- You likely already have deep product knowledge, you have the execution ability, and you have people skills as a result of working with other product managers, designers, and engineers. Many product designers and engineers in some way have worked hand in hand with product managers. You have an ability to understand what product managers do, and as a product manager, you will be able to empathize with designers and engineers better. For designers and engineers, these experiences are your superpowers.

- If you come from a design or engineering background, it can be immensely useful to have that prior context in a product management job. These are core skills that help build a product. You may have helped define the vision for a product, debated trade-offs, conducted user research, implemented designs, iterated on an existing product, and more. We will go over in a future chapter how having a design or engineering background can be beneficial when you become a product manager.

If you are in sales, customer success, or marketing:

- You understand customers. Sales, customer success, and marketing teams consistently interact with their customers directly or indirectly. They understand customer needs and behaviors in a way that would be highly translatable to product management.

- In sales, you are knowledgeable about the product and "sell" it to potential customers. Sales teams are always talking to customers. In sales, you know your customers' pain points and what their needs are. Sales teams know what it takes to land a customer or what may be a missed opportunity. They develop an intuitive understanding of their customers and help them understand why a product or service can solve their problems.

- In customer success, you are a product expert. You help your current customers "succeed" by helping them use the product and identifying how they can use the product to reach their goals. You optimize for their user experience as well as help retain them. Customer success managers often work hand in hand with product managers at startups. It is your job to talk with product managers about customer feedback.

- If you are in marketing, you are pitching the company and its services: its products, people, the overall value proposition, and more. In marketing, you develop a deep understanding of different markets, niches, and customers. You are constantly thinking about how to market a product or new feature. You are running campaigns, creating content, and more. Marketers typically run paid advertising and social campaigns towards their target customers. These are all critical skills for product managers, who constantly think about their products and the messages they want to convey.

- All of these roles interact with product managers and are immensely valuable. In product management, you need to know the customer deeply in order to understand how to build the right product and sell the right vision to your customers. Working in sales, customer success, and marketing all give you a deep understanding of your customers and help you develop the ability to sell products and services. Startups are at the intersection of building and selling. As a startup product manager, you are responsible for thinking about how to build and how to sell. Any of these roles will position you well for a career in product management at a startup.

If you are a data scientist:

- You are analytical and solve problems with data. Especially at startups, someone with an inclination for data and analytics is a value add. I hear the argument that there is not "enough" data at early stage companies and often it is based on intuition and experience. Likely, you will consider joining a startup that is close to finding product-market fit at scale or is still figuring that out. You are absolutely valuable. Data helps startups make sense of the unknown. Using data, you can identify what is and what is not working at a startup. You can quantify these product insights. Data scientists have directly translatable skills to product management. You have exercised product skill sets. You understand how metrics relate to customers, how data then influences prioritization decisions, and how to make sense out of random data. You also determine outcomes of product experiments, and more. Data is important at startups. These skills and experiences as a data scientist are directly related to how you will think strategically as a startup product manager.

If you are in another role:

- Many of you reading this may be in an entirely different role that feels unrelated to product management at first glance. This is where the Product Trifecta comes into play that we mentioned above. You need to think about how you have exercised Product Expertise, Product Strategy & Execution, and Product Soft Skills in the past. Either in your current role or in your previous role, you likely have had experiences that you can relate to those three buckets of skills. You may not be a "product manager" on paper, but you have built skills over time that a product manager also would have. It may not identically be what a product manager does day to day, but there are related experiences that are similar to what product managers do day to day. You may have experienced at least a few of the skills that are mentioned in this list. You need to frame your resume and your elevator pitch in the right way for product management roles. We will cover more of this soon and walk through how you can frame your experiences in the context of startup product management..

If you have not had a formal role **but** have built businesses or side projects before:

- This is especially helpful for students, entrepreneurs, or professionals that come from other backgrounds. I recommend you read an upcoming chapter that goes over why you should build a business as a new or aspiring product manager. It is important to remember that everything starts small. You can start with a small business and take it step by step over time to grow your business. That is what startup product management is. You start small, and then slowly, your growth compounds over time. Eventually, if you keep going, you will succeed and fail. If you learn from your failures, you can continue to grow that business over time. Learning how to build a business, regardless of whether you succeed or fail, will fundamentally teach you how to build startups and be a startup product manager.

If you have not had any internships or related roles at companies:

- You may be a student or a professional looking to make the switch into product management at a startup. These next few steps and questions would be valuable for you to understand how you can become a product manager. First, think about what you have been involved in at school or outside of work. Have you been a leader? Have you been part of an organization? Have you led cross-functional teams or worked with multiple stakeholders? Have you solved a problem and acted on it? Have you volunteered to do something? Have you planned an event? Have you worked in a customer-facing role or sold anything? Have you written about your experiences? Have you created content on a social platform and thought about how it solves a problem for an end user? It can be anything. These are all skills that product managers employ on a day to day basis. Startup product managers wear many hats, and likely, there have been a few experiences you have had that relate to product management. A helpful exercise would be to write down all of your previous experiences, branch out a few keywords of skills you used in those experiences, and relate them back to the skills in the Product Trifecta. You can position these past experiences in a way that can show you are capable of the role.

Note: we will talk more about writing effective cold emails in the next chapter! This will help you land your next role.

The Recipe for Writing an Effective Resume

1. Understand the Ingredients for Writing an Effective Product Manager Resume

You **do not** need a product management role to write a resume for product management roles. Your resume sets the narrative. It is important that you own the story and narrative. Believe in yourself and what you have done. This is how you market yourself to become a startup product manager. You need to think from the perspective of a founder, recruiter, or headhunter. They want to see relevant experiences to product management on your resume. You should make one resume specifically for startup product management roles.

I want to preface this by saying the following: I will give a few resources below, but a product manager resume must be tailored to your experiences. It must be personalized. Ideally, you have an old resume to work off of. Then it is just a matter of fine-tuning your existing resume rather than creating one from scratch.

Every bullet point on your resume matters. Each one should highlight impact quantitatively (metrics) or qualitatively (initiatives or projects that you led). Every bullet point should try to relate to one of the many specific skills in the Product Trifecta. A practical way to generate ideas for framing the content of your bullet points can be to look at sample job descriptions for product management roles at startups. This can help inspire ideas for how you can talk about your experiences in a way that aligns with the language of product management.

- Y Combinator's startup job board can be a great place to begin and find job descriptions for startup product management roles: https://www.ycombinator.com/jobs/role/product-manager

As a whole, you should be able to convey that you have a multi-faceted skillset, can work as an independent contributor, lead cross-functional teams, work with data, handle ambiguity, talk to customers, and consistently iterate on your projects to improve them. This is not an exhaustive list, and I highly recommend that you continue to view existing job descriptions. It is vital that you do research and begin to pattern match common trends for what startups are looking for when they hire a startup product manager. It can be personally valuable for you to understand the day to day responsibilities of a startup product manager and get familiarized with the commonalities of the role across different types of companies.

One important step of this chapter is to consider how your resume looks. This is a high-impact action item you can work on, and it often is not mentioned explicitly. You should modernize your resume for startups. Specifically, if you have a traditional resume, you need to update the visual design of your resume. Your resume should showcase a mix of your professionalism and creativity. There are several templates available through Figma that you can use. I would highly recommend using templates that Figma offers to build a more creative and product-focused resume.

- Figma Resume Templates: In order to find a great resume on Figma, I recommend searching "Product Resume" on Figma. You can use a resume template for product managers or product designers. I would suggest looking for a resume with a clean and minimalist aesthetic. You can save a template to your drafts and then continue to use that file to iterate on your resume over time whenever you need to update it.

Another important step is to look at examples of resumes. I recommend that you go beyond the advice I provide you here and review the components of building a great product manager resume from other product managers as well. It is important to understand patterns on what works well as well as what does not. You need to put your product manager hat on and do market research on resumes that have worked well. Below, I have a list of videos you can reference that are made by amazing creators who have provided free resources for you to reference. They provide detailed instructions on their perspectives for building product management resumes. Note: This is a great starting point, but you need to take it a step further. Anything you watch below should give you an initial set of ideas. The next step would be to align these learnings with your takeaways from the Product Trifecta we discussed earlier and any job descriptions that you see for product manager roles at startups.

- *Exponent: How to Write the Perfect Product Manager PM Resume | Tips & Steps*
- *Chloe Shih: Resume tips that got me my first Product Manager job*
- *Dr Nancy Li: Must Have Product Manager Resume Keywords Leading To PM Interviews*
    - I highly recommend you hone in on the concept of product manager keywords. This reiterates my suggestion of relating your skills to the Product Trifecta.

- *Diego Granados: How to create a Product Manager Resume*

Beyond the videos listed above, as mentioned before, you can also look at sample job descriptions as well. I would synthesize the learnings you find from YouTube with the job descriptions you find for product management roles at startups. Y Combinator's list of product management jobs at startups will be sufficient to give you ideas on common trends on what hiring managers look for in a startup product manager. Further, as we discussed in an earlier chapter, you can find more startup product manager roles by doing the following: reviewing additional startup job boards to find product manager jobs, subscribing to startup newsletters to see a weekly list of opportunities, and visiting venture capital firms' websites to see their portfolio companies who are hiring.

The criteria for what startups look for is different from what larger tech companies look for, so you will need to identify the differences and fill in the gaps. I am also happy to connect and provide 1:1 personalized feedback on how to create an effective resume. Please feel free to reach out for advice as well.

As we continue to build upon the concept of the Product Trifecta mentioned earlier, I would recommend that you highlight a few key qualities in your experiences. Whether you come from a product management background or not, you need to show you are customer focused and a problem solver. Your experiences need to emphasize your ability to be action oriented and solve high priority problems that people have. You can do this by quantifying impact through metrics and using product keywords. I would continue to reference the Product Trifecta and identify how the bullet points from each of experiences can be bucketed into the three categories. Precisely evaluate your current resume and think through every detail of how you can craft it in a way to be more impact focused while weaving in the core themes of product management.

Now, after reading this chapter, you can start to understand how you frame your background in a way that relates more effectively to product management. It is important to craft a narrative on why you are uniquely positioned to become a startup product manager. Also, you have learned how to write an effective resume that you can use to break into product management. The resume is the initial screening, but there is more to pitching yourself than a resume. Being able to talk to a founder and startup directly, in my opinion, has the greatest impact. The human connection you develop with someone and genuine alignment you feel with the mission of a company will matter the most.

The next chapter is crucial to understanding **how to reach out** to startups and founders. Cold-emailing is a skill that will help you not only with your startup search but also in many other facets of your life. You need to be proactive in advocating for yourself, marketing your brand, and launching your career to the next level. I will go over the effective strategies that have worked for me in landing multiple roles in product management. Knowing how to write an email well is important. It can help you develop relationships with founders and assist you in finding your next product role at a startup.

CHAPTER 6

THE COLD EMAIL THAT HELPED ME LAND MY FIRST FULL-TIME PRODUCT MANAGER ROLE

Cold emailing is one of the most critical, impactful, and actionable steps you can take in your journey to becoming a startup product manager. Many of you who are reading this will have to send a cold email in order to land a startup product manager role. Cold emailing is one of the best things you can do. You get to take the first step in achieving your goals. You get to take initiative and take control of your journey. A large proportion of the founders you email **will** respond if you write your email well. Whether that leads to a call, an interview, on-going mentorship, an exchange of ideas, a startup product manager role, or a referral to another founder, you should always take the time to put yourself out there. The serendipity lies in connecting with others. You never know where your next call will bring you. Cold emailing, when done well, is substantially more effective than sending your resume somewhere or applying on job boards. The more you differentiate yourself from the norm, the more opportunities you will find. This may be the one of the most important chapters in this book and give you what you are looking for. Cold emailing can help you land your first or next role in product management as a new or aspiring product manager. In order to land your first role in startup product management, you not only need to send a cold email out but also find someone who believes in your ability to succeed on the job.

How To Find Someone Who Believes In You

1. Landing Your First Role in Product Management Requires Someone to Make a Bet on You

Breaking into product management was not easy for me, but through my learnings, I will try my best to make it easier for you. One of the most important takeaways I received from the process of finding startup product management roles is that you have to believe in yourself first. Once you believe in yourself, you can then find someone who believes in you. Even if you are 50% of the way there and do not feel confident 100% of the time in your search, you have to pick yourself back up and keep going. You have to believe you are a product manager before you are a product manager. Be confident in your abilities and who you are. Consistency is the most important part, especially when it comes to cold emailing. In order to land a startup product management role, you need to believe in yourself enough that you can trust the process and that you **will** find a founder who believes in you as well.

We have established that getting into product management requires someone to make a bet on you. The question is — how do you get someone to bet on **you**?

The truth is — if you are reading this, you **are** capable. You have the curiosity to become a startup product manager. You have come this far because you have an interest and commitment to your career goals, as well as your ability to succeed in product management. With an initial belief, anything is possible. If you can visualize where you want to be, you now just need to take the actions to get there. You just need to put the work in, and the results will come. You must work to develop the core skills a product manager needs. We already covered in previous chapters how you may have translatable past experiences to startup product management. You need to frame your skills within the Product Trifecta and pitch yourself as someone who is ready to take on a startup product manager role.

If you want to go above and beyond, there are a few more practical ways to develop the skills a startup product manager needs to have. This will even help you further on the job as a product manager. Frankly, if you are able to excel in any of these areas, you will become a startup product manager. Founders want to hire individuals who can do these well because this is what they are looking for when hiring a product manager.

If you wanted the secret recipe, this is it. Learning any combination of these skills can help more effectively pitch you for startup product manager roles and also make you better on the job. These are the skills: writing, communicating verbally, understanding and applying the design process, building side projects either through designing or coding, and starting a business. Please take a look the following chapters for more context into why these are valuable skills:

- *"Why Writing is Your Ultimate Strength as a Startup Product Manager."*
- *"The Power of Verbal Communication For Startup Product Managers."*
- *"Why Learning to Design and Code Are Superpowers For Startup Product Managers."*
- *"Why You Should Build a Business as a Product Manager."*

The Cold Email That Helped me Land a Product Manager Role

2. The Cold Email That Helped me Land my First Full-Time Product Manager Role at a Startup

The email below helped me land my first full-time role in product management at a startup. Now, this is a great **starting point**. We will go over the secrets I have on how to write a better cold email later on. I believe you can write a significantly more effective cold email, and we will go step by step on how you can do so.

Product Manager & Designer External » Inbox ×

Manan Modi <mnm67@cornell.edu>
to hiring ▾

Hi there,

I hope you are doing well. My name is Manan, and I have experience within Product & Design. I resonated with the work your team is doing within the FinTech space and saw that you were looking for people to join your team. Attached is my updated resume. Thank you!

Featured work: https://www.linkedin.com/feed/update/urn:li:activity:6759505820184137728/
Product & Design work: https://medium.com/design-bootcamp/a-new-way-to-learn-robinhood-case-study-2f9df0fa1868
Product & Design work: https://medium.com/design-bootcamp/cocreate-fostering-a-community-of-students-launching-creative-projects-10b4c00c1354
Website: mananmodi.com

Best,
Manan Modi
--
Cornell University
The ILR School | mananmodi.com
(908)-342-4092 | mnm67@cornell.edu | LinkedIn

To preface, cold-emailing can be helpful for the following reasons:

1. It will help you develop relationships with founders and product teams at startups. The startup world is small in the sense that you are playing in a long term game, and likely you will come across many of these startup team members again in the future. Starting to develop relationships with startups can be a great way to open doors for you in the future, and you can also open doors for other people.

2. It will help you find a product role or product-adjacent role at a startup. Cold emails are the most effective way to get your foot in the door and allow you to advocate for yourself. You can go straight to the leaders of a company and show you can provide value. Through the calls that you set up with founders, a few founders may find that you are a great fit for their startups and offer you opportunities to join.

3. It will open doors for you beyond what we mention here. As mentioned before, serendipity lies in connecting with others. You truly never know where connecting with a startup or a founder will lead you. The more people you connect with, the more opportunities you will find. You have to remember that it is a two-way street. Everytime you successfully prove you can provide value, you will find pockets of opportunity where others may reciprocate and provide value back to you.

There are a few more secrets I have for cold emailing. These strong recommendations will help you tailor your cold emails effectively and take them to the next level.

Seven Secret Steps to Writing an Effective Cold Email

3. How to Write a Better Cold Email

1. **Keep it concise.** The cold email I wrote was around two lines on my desktop. Try making it even shorter than that — this is your first impression, and you need to show you can be direct and articulate as a product manager. Use your cold email as a way to communicate your interests, value, and authenticity.

2. **Personalize it.** If you are reaching out to someone, say "Hi [*insert first name of founder*]," at the beginning.

   a. There are a few ways to further personalize an email:

i.   You can specifically say why **you** are interested in the company and their mission. This may align with your previous experiences or with your values, and you want to hone in on this. You can create a personal connection with their company's mission or goals and communicate that.

ii. You can talk about why the founder's background intrigued you. There may be a set of experiences they had that you resonated with, ie) they may be an alumni, they may have gone down a similar career path, they are from the same area, they have similar interests, etc.

iii. You can mention if there was a project they worked on that caught your interest. There may be a product, set of features, or services they launched that particularly caught your attention. You can highlight why this project struck a chord with you and why it relates to your career ambitions in a concise, professional email.

Now, the wording in my email was a bit vague and could have improved in terms of personalization. I said: "I resonated with the work your team is doing within the FinTech space." This is not the best way to approach a company. Ask yourself a few questions. Do you have a suggestion for their product? Have you used the product and gained any insights? What about their mission resonates with you? Have you read any articles or watched any videos on the company? Answer these questions and incorporate them into your outreach as well.

3. Get their attention in the subject line. People are busy. Founders are definitely busy. You need to grab their attention quickly and creatively. I said "Product Manager & Designer" in my header because I previously did part-time work in product management and also created design case studies. I knew that I had some foundational skills, though I did not have full-time experience yet. Now, this is up to you in terms of how you grab their attention. I recommend that you pitch yourself as who you will become. You should make it about who you will become because it will relate to the founder: they are already looking to hire individuals who can add value, as well as bring a positive mindset. You have to believe you are already there. You may want to concisely highlight in the subject line one or more of the following: your skills, your role, the impact you can make, something unique about the founder, or anything else. There are many ways to grab the attention of a founder in the email. Do what feels right to you, and iterate from there.

4. **Show you can add value.** This, in my opinion, is the most important part. You add value by **showing your skills**. When communicating your experiences and skills, you need to be persuasive.

b. This can be done by incorporating the three pillars of persuasion: pathos, ethos, logos.

    i.   Pathos is the ability to persuade through an emotional connection. You need to tie in your skills and experiences to the mission of the company. Figure out how your "why" aligns with the company's "why" and the founder's "why." When you discover your intrinsic "why" for doing something, you will naturally be more passionate about the startup if it aligns with your mission. Joining a startup and being part of this world is about finding a mission that you genuinely care about. Despite the ups and downs, you will be less likely to waver and more likely to keep going in your journey as a startup product manager. It is crucial to convey your emotional connection to why you want to be a product manager at a startup.

    ii.   Ethos is the ability to persuade through your authority on the subject and credibility. In my cold email, I said I had experience in "Product & Design." I showed these skills by providing links to two design case studies I previously created. I used ethos to add additional layers: my email talked about how I was featured by a product manager on LinkedIn (Lewis C. Lin), and I gave them my personal website. I used social proofing as a way to show that I was ready for the role. Your cold email is a form of marketing. You need to capitalize on your prior experiences and vouch for yourself. Have you worked for a company backed by venture investors? Did you work on any high impact projects with customers? Can you talk about any brands to help grab attention? Has your work been featured anywhere? Are there projects you can share? These are all great additions to talk about yourself if any apply to you. However, it has to be subtle. There is a balance you have to have – it can be a great line or introduction to reference a few names, but you cannot make it your full email. Alternatively, even if you feel like you cannot use ethos effectively yet, it is not necessary to utilize it. Eventually, in your career, you will be able to. It is important that you can use it effectively now that you do it in your cold email.

iii. Logos is the ability to persuade through your reasoning capabilities and logic. In order to use logos in your cold email, you need to reverse engineer how startups work and understand what founders need. Startups have limited capital and resources to hire talent. Founders have limited time and energy, and hiring is one of the many responsibilities they have. As a result, they need to hire individuals who can wear multiple hats and do their job well. If you personally enjoy wearing multiple hats, you should appeal to this because the founder always has gaps they need to fill. My first full-time startup product management role ended up being primarily in product management, but I did take on other responsibilities that were outside of traditional "product management." Showing that you have another skillset (design, marketing, coding, etc) is valuable. It is also a smaller risk that the business has to take on hiring you because you have the ability to pivot if need be. It means you can learn multiple things and be scrappy. This is important at a startup. In your initial cold emails or conversations with founders, if you can highlight your ability to wear multiple hats and prove it, you will be successful in your outreach.

5. **Ask them to connect.** The way that I would approach a cold email is to think of yourself as a salesperson for your career. You need to creatively think about how you can convert your emails to conversations. The more conversations you have, the more chance of success (however you define it) you will have: whether it is building relationships, landing an interview for a role, learning more about the founder's story, connecting to find a partner in the startup space, or anything else. You need to have a

specific "ask" in your email. My recommendation is to say it explicitly because founders are reading through several emails all the time, and they cannot directly assume your intent. You can also try creative ways to be implicit in your ask to connect. I have seen it work both ways. In my cold email, I casually said that I "saw that you were looking for people to join your team." In your email, you can include that and also ask the question: "do you have a few minutes to connect?" You would ask for a few minutes of their time after you have included the strategies we discussed before to write an effective cold email. At the end, you can say: "thank you for your time." You need to proactively think about the different components we discussed for a cold email and how you will implement them. Once you begin to ask explicitly or implicitly to connect with a founder, you will begin to see many more cold emails convert and lead to a conversation with the founder.

6. **Follow up.** There may be times when founders miss your cold email. Do not take it personally. If you follow up, you can have a second or third chance to potentially connect with a founder. If you are truly passionate about a company and a role, you can try sending a kind follow-up email a week later. You can quickly reiterate the important pieces of what you mentioned before and ask to meet. Also, when you do meet with a founder, you can follow up after that call. Whether you are reaching out for the first

time or sending an email after meeting with them, you should be respectful of their time and not send too many emails.

7. **Be curious.** One of the most important parts of your cold email is to let your curiosity authentically shine through. Your tone should be more diplomatic and curious, instead of immediately sending your resume. You do not need to send your resume immediately. Projects or work samples can be helpful to convey your interest. You can mention your intent and be direct, without sending your resume. If you are excited about the product, mission, team, or anything else — focus on that. You can provide thoughtful suggestions on the product, talk about how you would envision the future of the product (be careful with being overly prescriptive), or ask them a question if you are curious. You can develop the relationship first and get to know the team before you say that you are applying for a role. This theme of providing value and showing value is a great way to get your foot in the door. If you want to become a startup product manager, you need to show that you can be one before you come one.

How to Connect With Any Startup Founder

4. How to Get in Touch With a Startup Founder

We have reviewed how to write a cold email and the basics around finding startups to join. Next, you need to be able to reach out to the founder. Cold emailing and reaching out of the blue is common in the startup world. Entrepreneurship is built on serendipitous moments. This can be done by finding a founder's email. Typically, a founder's email address can be found online. You can also guess a founder's email: it is likely *firstname@company.com.*

We can go over an example together:

- You are emailing a founder named "Rohan," and he currently is a co-founder at a startup called "Music Artists." Musicartists.com is the domain name you found on Google. You can likely try "rohan@musicartists.com" as the email address. You *may* be able to verify this on the company website or on their LinkedIn profile. In short: founders typically list their email address somewhere, and if not, you guess it.

There are also other ways to get in touch with a startup team:

- Alternatively, you can find an email to contact the team directly on the website. There may be an HR or hiring email on the website. In this example, you would go to musicartists.com and check out the "About," "Contact," or other sections on the company website.

- Most venture-backed startups you will find today have at least two co-founders. You can always try emailing the other co-founders as well. You may have found that there are two founders for Music Artists: "Rohan" and "Cam." You can email "cam@musicartists.com" if you want to reach out.

- There are other ways to get in touch with a founder beyond emailing them. You can try connecting on Twitter or LinkedIn and write a short message as well.

- As mentioned before, you now know that every venture capital firm has a set of startups in their portfolio. Venture investors are always trying to be the matchmakers with their portfolio: they want to match great talent with their startups to help them succeed. If you search for a startup on Crunchbase, you can find almost any startup's publicly listed investors. You may be able to find the individual(s) who invested in the startup from that specific firm, either on Crunchbase or through a quick Google search. Once you know the venture firm that invested and the name of the investor from the firm, you can reach out to the investor over email. You can always reach out to a VC who has this startup in their portfolio. They may even send you other portfolio company opportunities if they find that you are a great match.

If none of these options work, you can try other creative options that you may think of. If you are excited about a company, you can find a way to nicely ask to get in touch and connect. You may be able to get an introduction from another person, create a design case study that redesigns an existing feature, offer to connect the startup with another startup if you see potential synergies, or anything else. There are multiple ways to get in touch with a startup team, and you can run a series of experiments to see what works and what does not work. Cold emailing, getting in touch with founders, and understanding how to develop relationships with startups are useful skills that will help you beyond even getting a startup product manager role. I highly recommend putting yourself out there. There is unlimited upside if you keep trying and believing in yourself.

Lastly, I recommend focusing both on the **quality** of your initial outreach and the **quantity** of your outreach with different companies. You need to write emails well to the companies you reach out to. You also need to reach out to **several** companies and aim for volume. You may or may not get an initial call or find that perfect fit with the first few companies you connect with. The important lesson is that you continue to learn from every email you send, every call you help, and every person you meet. Keep going!

Now, you know the secrets on how to cold email startups and founders. The next chapter will focus on how you find and identify the startups to join. This will go more in-depth into evaluating startups and opportunities for your career. I will provide a due diligence playbook you can use to evaluate startups to join. **Finding the right** fit is the most important decision you can make when considering a startup, especially as a product manager.

CHAPTER 7

THE STEP-BY-STEP PLAYBOOK YOU CAN USE TO EVALUATE STARTUPS TO JOIN

Earlier, we went over how you can find startups and the different channels you can find them through. Now, how do you truly evaluate a startup? You are probably thinking the following: *startups are risky, but I want to be on a rocketship or any fast-paced company that has a lot of upside and will allow me to grow.* I want to provide a due diligence playbook to evaluate startups to join as a new or aspiring startup product manager. Having worked as an early stage product manager, I can give the playbook for everything I have learned. Together, we can help you discover your next startup product manager role more effectively through this process.

The Keys to Product-Market Fit

1. The Stages of Product-Market Fit

First, one of the most valuable insights you can have into a startup's trajectory is knowing the stage of product-market fit it is at. *What is product-market fit?* Product-market fit happens when a product solves a need in the market: customers would want to buy, use, and talk about a company's product. Importantly, the customers consciously make a purchase decision to spend money on this product. Customers also come back to this product, and they would have strong usage of the product. This impact on the customer must be great enough that the startup begins to formulate a business model based on this demand. The product can become a true solution for a need that exists in the market. Joining a startup that is close to finding product-market fit, has found product-market fit, or is finding product-market fit at scale is a very important decision to make as a new or aspiring startup product manager.

"For a company to grow really big, it must (a) make something lots of people want, and (b) reach and serve all those people." — Paul Graham, Founder of Y Combinator.
http://www.paulgraham.com/growth.html

Startups that are venture-backed typically go through several stages of venture funding before going public. For most startups, you can broadly correlate product-market fit with the venture funding stages of startups (Pre-seed, Seed, Series A, Series B, Series C, and beyond). To understand how product-market fit relates to funding stages, you can read the explanation below. Please read my note below after these bullet points as well.

- **Pre-PMF: Pre-Seed, Seed, (sometimes Series A)** — Startups are at pre-product-market fit in these early stages. This means that a startup has not found product-market fit yet. Startups are typically experimenting at these stages to determine their business models. They may have a minimum viable product (MVP), or the product is still an idea or concept at this point. The overall business strategy and product vision are also more frequently shifting around. *There are, however, exceptions as mentioned later below.* In terms of what this means for you as a startup product manager, you will likely spend most of your time focused on customer discovery or testing out new ideas: these new ideas may either come from the founders, and you also have to identify opportunities to grow the company. The founders are focused very much on the product, and revenues are not at a point yet where they can begin hiring many employees. They are just beginning to form their product team.

- **PMF: Series A** — Startups that raise a Series A generally have very early product-market fit. They have typically found their early customers. However, startups at this stage have not typically found wide-scale adoption yet. They are almost there. At this stage, they do have enough funding or traction to begin hiring a few product managers. These startup product managers will play a critical role in scaling the company to product-market fit at scale and consecutive rounds of financing. The revenue and growth gap between Series A and B is one of the most challenging to close, and this gap differentiates companies that find early product-market fit versus product-market fit at scale. When a startup initially reaches product-market fit, the company must focus on finding more customers and having a clear growth strategy. Startup product managers are perfect at this stage. They can help define the product portfolio, run experiments with new features, work on the highest priority initiatives, and have wide-reaching impacts across the company. Founders traditionally hire startup product managers at this stage because it is time for them to begin to delegate product execution more to other employees. The product vision will change, but it should change less so compared to earlier stages. The founders should have an understanding of prioritization at this point and have a focused business plan in order to get to the next level of revenue, which will help them raise a Series B. If the founders consistently switch their business strategy at this point, it can be a sign of adaptability but also a red flag to look out for. When a startup reaches product-market fit and raises a Series A, it is important to focus. Startup product managers should help define and know the exact objectives and key metrics on a quarterly basis. These would tie into the targets that the company has to hit. You should focus your due diligence on also identifying if the startup has a culture of focus and accountability. Startup product managers should not be working on everything but only on initiatives that move the needle forward. The company should be tracking metrics relevant to its business model. At this stage, startup product managers will be able to align with their executives on clear north stars for the company. A north star metric essentially helps align the product, design, engineering, and business teams on a common goal. At the early stages of product-market fit you may have multiple products to manage across the startup. However, you need to focus on the most important one or two. Startup product management is a balancing act between focusing on the north star and also experimenting on further initiatives on the side. This is why I typically recommend it to many product managers who want to optimize for career growth and overall upside. However, startups with early product-market fit can be riskier than later stage startups that have clearly established product-market fit. It is especially critical to evaluate the founding team. The founders' decisions make or break early stage startups. The most important qualities to look out founders at this stage involve the following: they should have an ability to prioritize initiatives, understand the best opportunities for their startup in the market they are operating in, work collaboratively with customers to understand their needs deeply, be unafraid to shift their business model in a thoughtful manner, hire the right operators without over-hiring, and learn to trust their teams at this stage by delegating execution. Startup product managers should be intentional about the teams and founders they join at this stage. Do your research. Joining a startup in its early stages of product-market fit can be one of the most exciting experiences for a product manager.

- **PMF at scale: Series B onwards** — At Series B, most startups are beginning to reach product-market fit at scale. Typically, at this stage and onwards, product-market fit has truly been validated. Many startups are ready to be on a breakout trajectory. There are exceptions, however, such as *Fast.*

  o Fast raised a $102 million Series B but never reached product-market fit at scale. They hired too many employees and did not have a scalable business model. As a result, they had to shut down operations. There are scenarios where a company has not found product-market fit at Series B onwards. This is a difficult situation. Companies sometimes raise capital at high valuations and then cannot justify the revenue and growth. This happens in certain situations. You have to be aware of them as a startup product manager when you are looking for roles. These situations are tricky. Premature rounds can make it increasingly difficult to raise a successive round, especially when a startup cannot justify it. Startups sometimes raise a lot of funding, do not meet revenue expectations, and cannot control their spending. They may look for more funding and a greater valuation, but this results in significant dilution if the next round of financing does come to fruition. ***You always need to ask questions and do your research.*** Regardless of the stage and your initial beliefs on product-market fit, you have to think critically about any startup opportunity you are offered. I always recommend doing your own due diligence on the founding team, the market they are operating in, their financials, and their growth metrics. Throughout this book, we have already covered many factors that you should consider and will continue to discuss more factors that you should consider when conducting due diligence.

Note: there are instances where you can find an early stage startup that has found deep product-market fit, but the team has chosen to <u>bootstrap</u> and not raise venture capital. This is great. Though most software startup founders that you will come across often raise venture funding, there are exceptions to this. There are diamonds in the rough that have found product-market fit at scale and have opted not to raise venture funding. These can be great opportunities because there generally may be less dilution compared to venture-backed startups. There is a greater likelihood you can get very meaningful equity in your compensation as a startup product manager. Also, you will learn how to fundamentally bootstrap a business and grow it without taking money from others. That is probably the most valuable learning you would have. Learning how to grow a company without venture funding is a unique opportunity to learn how to build a business, without capital from investors that would facilitate growth. Instead, you would see first-hand how a company organically grows and how it reinvest its profits towards future growth. As a startup product manager, you would learn how to become a great strategist and capital allocator through these experiences.

Now, you are probably wondering: *what types of startups would I recommend to most people to join?* Well, it depends. For most, I would recommend joining a startup that has at least found early product-market fit, has a great founding team that you believe in, and has raised enough capital from investors. Also, if you can find a bootstrapped startup with product-market fit, you can go for product management roles at these companies as well. Ultimately, you need to determine what you value as a person and that will help you choose the best role for you as a startup product manager.

- The only thing that matters by Marc Andreessen: https://pmarchive.com/guide_to_startups_part4.html

To summarize what we discussed earlier, product-market fit usually happens at Series A and Series B. There are situations where product-market fit can occur before Series A. Pre-product-market fit with low funding can be rocky, and it is much more uncertain. Series B is typically where the product market fit continues to show even more.

The inflection point is where capital injections from further rounds helps solidify the growth of the company and its team.

For most new and aspiring PMs, joining a company at a later round can involve more mentorship opportunities, better onboarding, and reaping the benefits of working at a fast-growing company. Ideally, early on, you join a founder that has had industry-specific experience targeting the space that you will be in or has had previous operating experience as a founder or PM. However, I do recommend trying a company at every early stage. All lessons are valuable.

There are success and failure stories at every stage of venture funding for startups. If you want to be on a rocketship, the Series B and C rounds onwards are typically the best to join if you are optimizing for financial upside. The financial upside at Series A is unpredictable, given that it is at very early levels of product-market fit. The financial upside may be more likely at Series B onwards startups that have found product-market fit at scale. While financial success is important, there are caveats to this. You may have to join multiple startups and wait several years for an exit to realize any financial gains for a startup. Financial upside can be valuable, but you still should look for startups based on what you truly want. You should have a set of core values and how you define success for yourself. You may want to optimize for career growth or working towards a mission you care about instead.

If you want to grow the most in your career, you should optimize for the type of role you will have, the founding team, who your manager will be, and the overall growth prospects of the company. Your career as a startup product manager can be defined by the industry you have an impact on, the types of customers you help, the people you meet along the way, and how you grow as a person. Ultimately, a startup product management role can be a stepping stone for becoming a successful founder one day, a startup advisor, an angel investor, or full-time venture investor. There is no right or wrong answer to this question of what stage of product-market fit you should join or what venture round you will join because there are unique things you will learn at every stage.

How to Analyze Product, Market, Team, And GTM of a Startup

2. Understand the Product, Market, Team, and Go-to-Market Strategy:

- **Product:** Some startups may not have a product yet, but if they do, you need to have high standards if they have one.

You need to be as critical and detail-oriented as possible when vetting the product. Yes, startups move quickly and products can change. But you need to holistically understand the product, both what works well and what does not work well. It is crucial to evaluate the user experience of the product. It has to be the best product on the market that solves a given user need or be on the road to becoming the best. You need to consider the differentiated value add it has in the market. Compare the product to competitor products. You need to analyze everything you can: everything from the website, to the sales demo, the user experience of the product, the visual design of the product, the channels that the product is marketed on, and the reviews of the product. If it is not the best product yet, do you have the best team that is capable of improving this product? You need to analyze the individuals who are building the product: the product team, design team, and engineering team. **Ask yourself:** after doing your own research, does the product make sense to you? Before you take on a startup product manager role, you need to use the product. Go through the end to end flow if you can or ask for a demo from the sales team. You need to reflect on how long it takes for you to "get" the product. You need to understand why this product is fundamentally important to its target customers. For most products that you see yourself working on, you need to have the self-awareness and the ability to check in with yourself to see if you would enjoy building this product further. As a startup product manager, you are the expert of the product. You have to understand why the product is important to the business. You have to understand how the product is used by customers and why it solves a product in the market. Is it a loved product? How difficult is it to build the product, and does it require deep industry experience to build it? Even if it does require industry experience, can you find a way to pick up that knowledge over time as a product manager? How do customers feel about the product? The last question is the most important. You can talk to customers or find product reviews, testimonials, and other resources online. You need to know **how** initial customers feel — they are the strongest advocates for the product.

- **Market:** the market that is one of the most important factors to evaluate. You need to understand the market that a startup is operating in, as well as the market that the product is built for. If you have a great product & team, you can still have poor market conditions that can still prevent both from succeeding. As a startup product manager, you should know the market in-and-out. It is a way for you to gauge the potential of the company. If a great team has a great product **and** they operate in a great market, there is a significant opportunity for you to find everything you may be looking for in a startup. Every ingredient is part of the recipe for a startup's success: the product, the market, and the team. **Ask yourself:** What is the market size? Who are the key players and competitors in the market? What is the difficulty of a new entry in the market? What power do the various stakeholders have in the market? Has there been consolidation or M&A activity? Have there been private equity roll-ups? Is the market cyclical in nature?

- **Team:** the team is perhaps the most important choice you can make from my experience. A startup will always pivot: the market will change, and the product will change. People will come and go, but the core team should usually stay intact for your first year. The executive team has the most influence on the strategic action the company takes. The second group with the most influence are the individuals who report directly to the executive team. Startup product managers early on report to the executive team, either the founders or the head of product. The founders and the team around the founders are imperative to get right when you pick a startup to join. **Ask yourself:** Who are the co-founders, what are their backgrounds, and are they former operators? Do they have industry experience? Do you believe in the founders' abilities to hire and retain talent? Do they have a strong technical, sales, or product background? If not, do they fill these gaps elsewhere? Do the founders have a track record; have they scaled and exited companies before? Do the founders have a strong reputation, and can they build and keep trust? What type of culture do they set? Do the founders have balance? What do they do outside of work? Is their main focus building the business? Would you see yourself working for them long-term or for multiple years? How will they help you get to where you want to be in your career? Why are they the best operators to succeed in this market? How large is the team? How does the executive team talk about each other, and how often do they talk to each other? Where did the founders hire the most, the least? What are the strengths and weaknesses that you can identify up front? Can you provide unique value as a startup product manager?

- **Go-to-Market:** Distribution is just as important as product. Distribution is important because you need people to use a product. You cannot rely on word of mouth as a growth strategy. For people to use the product, your marketing has to be hands-on. Once you build a functioning and working product that your core users love, you will need to have a strong go-to-market function: sales, marketing, customer success, and more. It is important to evaluate a startup's go-to-market function. ***Ask yourself:*** how are the sales, marketing, growth, and customer success teams structured? How do they experiment? Is there a data-driven culture? Do they have a clear content strategy? Does the company have a content schedule and post content consistently? What channels do they market across? Check the startup's social media channels: YouTube, Twitter, LinkedIn Facebook, Product Hunt, Instagram, TikTok, etc. Do they run paid ads? How would economic trends affect their ad spend and social campaigns? For instance, in highly cyclical markets such as lending or real estate, the market conditions could impact a startup's ad spend during economic downturns. How does the startup talk to customers? What differentiates this startup's GTM function as a whole? Who leads each team within the GTM function, and what are their backgrounds? What have these teams done so far that you can see? What feedback have customers or prospective customers left online? What are the product ratings across various channels? Who has the startup partnered with? Are there strong network effects for this startup? How does this startup's marketing efforts compare to other competitors' marketing efforts?

Aligning With The Startup Mission

3. Aligning With the Mission of a Startup:

Startups can be purposeful and create meaning for you. Startups are known for helping you grow your career, providing you with endless learning opportunities, enabling you to find like-minded operators, inspiring you to challenge the status-quo, facilitating your ability to take risks, encouraging you to experiment, and more. Most importantly, startups help you align your work with your purpose. As a startup product manager, you will be working long hours. You will have an array of responsibilities. During those hours, you will have to think critically about your product, customers, prioritization, execution, competitors, and so much more. Given that you will spend a significant proportion of your time working, why not work for a startup that aligns with who you are? Throughout your career, you may care about the type of impact you want to have in the world. You may have a passion for certain things. Most of your day will be spent working, so why not work on a mission that you care about? Startups give you the chance to find something that inspires childlike curiosity in you. They give you the chance to find something that motivates you to get up in the morning. Your first opportunity may not be perfect. Startup product managers get to wear so many hats that you get a taste of everything: you will discover what you love to work on. Eventually, you will find a startup opportunity that aligns with your passion or helps you find it. If anything, becoming a startup product manager will provide you with the toolkit and skillset to strategically execute on problems that you care about. In the future, you can continue to solve challenging problems that excite you as a startup product manager, founder, investor, or in any other role..

Startup product managers have different archetypes and interests, and a lot of people care about the mission of the company they work for. When you understand *why* you are doing something, you can always figure out *how* you will achieve it when working alongside others. You need to find a culture that inspires you.

"Culture eats strategy for breakfast" — Peter Drucker.
https://www.managementcentre.co.uk/management-consultancy/culture-eats-strategy-for-breakfast/

In order to identify if you align with the culture and mission of a startup, you need to reflect on who you are. You can ask yourself the following questions: why do I want to become a product manager? Why do I want to join a startup or go into tech? Is this a problem-space that I deeply care about? Do I resonate with the story of the company?

Maslow's Hierarchy of Needs can be a great framework to understand why it is important to work on a mission that resonates with you. Your identity does not have to be your work. However, you may spend 40 of your waking hours a week working at a job. You should enjoy it and try to find fulfillment in what you do! Working at a venture-backed startup is great, and if it can help inspire purpose in you through a clear mission, it will make the journey much more fulfilling and valuable to you.

The Risk-Return Secrets of Evaluating Venture-Backed Startups

4. Do Your Research on Venture-Backed Startups:

Investing your time and energy into researching venture-backed startups will pay off when you search for new opportunities as a startup product manager. The upfront research you conduct is critical. You want to join a startup that has a product, team, and market that you believe in. I want to help you succeed, especially early on in your career. You gain valuable lessons from learning, failing and growing at a startup. Ideally, if it is your first startup, you should look for a startup that has a level of stability despite its fast-paced nature and challenges. In a previous chapter, we went over how startups can be at different stages of product-market fit and how this relates to the different stages of venture funding. Startup stability is often defined by the level of product-market fit, the amount raised, and the runway period. At some point in your career, I do think it is equally valuable to work at a startup that is bootstrapped. As mentioned before, a bootstrapped startup will help you understand what it takes to scale a company without funding. There are ways to minimize the monetary risks that you individually take on by going to a startup. Whether a startup is venture-backed or bootstrapped, you should ask yourself a few questions. How much funding does this startup have? How long will their funding last? How fast is their revenue growing? How many employees do they have? What is their overall cost structure? Do they have low cash burn proportional to the revenue they are generating? You need to especially do due diligence on the monetary risks associated with any startup opportunity.

The reason I say this is because **90% of startups fail**. Most startups fail due to a lack of product-market fit, or they run out of funding.

See the following resources for context:

- *https://nanoglobals.com/startup-failure-rate-myths-origin/*
- Harj Taggar - Why Do Startups Fail

The secret to understanding risk-return is to look for startups that have a baseline level of stability yet the potential for upside. In short, you should look for startups that understand their market well, have started to gain a competitive position, are intentional with who they hire, and have disciplined spending. Granted, there is no right or wrong answer to finding the **right** startup. I am a proponent of going to venture-backed startups that have some level of product-market fit.

You should know the following about venture-backed startups:

1. Having multiple well-known VCs back a startup is a signal that it has promise, but you always need to do your own due diligence. There are startups that had the best investors and still failed. The power law of venture capital is important to understand: most startups will fail, but a few startups out of the many investments made will

succeed and return value that is more than enough to make up for the losses. A rule of thumb is to do your own research and see if the startup aligns with your values. If a startup has great investors on top of that, it can help solidify your belief in the startup. Look for VC firms that have a reputation of strong due diligence.

2. The brands of the venture firms who invested in your startup can be beneficial for future career transitions. The venture firms who back the startups you work for can be important early on in your career if you want to pivot. Once you have been in a role, you can say a variation of *"I worked for a Sequoia-backed startup as the second full-time PM. I helped build logistics and payment infrastructure that allowed B2B customers to purchase products internationally with fast and affordable delivery."* There are founders, VCs, and product managers that use this strategy of brand association. It can give you flexibility and open doors. If you were at a startup for at least a year, you invested your energy into building a company and maneuvered through highs & lows. When you put your blood, sweat, and tears into building something, you deserve to vouch for yourself and use brand associations to further your own brand. You can craft a compelling case for yourself when finding your next opportunity. Pitching yourself is part of the game. You should always vouch for yourself effectively. Finding startup product management roles is an end-to-end

process. It involves developing relationships, finding a true fit for yourself, conveying your value to a startup, and **signaling and marketing.** You need to learn how to send brand signals and believe in yourself. Market yourself as a great startup product manager to any company you are joining. You do not have to attach yourself to a brand or single identity forever, but brand associations can propel your career in helpful ways. Be your biggest promoter.

3. The venture firms who back a startup early on can have an impact on the venture firms who invest later. Having a few big names on a startup's cap table is not a deal breaker, but it can go a long way in ensuring the startup raises another round. If the startup can live up to or exceed expectations of early investors **and** they are backed by top investors, you can be confident that there will be inbound demand to invest in the startup. Assuming this is true, there will be investors rushing to invest in the startup before talks of the next round even start. If a startup was backed by Sequoia, a16z, Acceel, or NEA at the seed round, they are already on the radars of many firms when it comes to raising a Series A. Now, there is no guarantee that the startup raises its next round when already backed by great investors. Having great investors back you early on can have a substantial impact on the perception a future investor has on the startup. There are exceptions to this, as there have been great investments passed on at every round by top

investors. For most startups, the firms who invest in them matter. If a recognizable venture firm is backing a startup, it catches attention. To summarize, the investors that a startup has early on can play to its advantage in raising another round. When a startup can raise another round, it can further fuel growth and have increased runway that can lead to further success.

4. You should go to a startup that does not burn significantly more than it generates in revenue. This sounds like common sense. If a startup raised a $10 million Series A, the startup should not be spending $4 million a year if they are only generating $500k in revenue a year. This means they are burning 8 times the amount they are earning. You always need to ask startups around their growth projections and what they can generate in revenue next year, as well as their cost structures. As another example, let's say you find another startup that is burning a lot less cash and generating more revenue. You need to check if they have enough runway for the next 12–24 months. If you are in a recession, you definitely need to know if they have enough runway for 24-36 months. Further, it is important to understand how much a startup plans to hire over the next few months. Hiring directly impacts costs the most, and it will help you understand how costs change over time. When you are evaluating a venture-backed startup, all of these factors around its financials will help you make

a better decision. Identifying the financial state of a startup early on saves you stress later. The current and future financial state of a startup will have implications for the company's success and your growth at the company. Do your due diligence. It helps you focus less on the "risk" you are taking when you join the startup and instead focus more on how you can help the startup succeed when you join. When you are worried less about the financial state, if you have done your research early on, you will have a greater capacity to focus on how you can continue to grow in your startup product manager career. However, even when you join a startup, you need to keep your investor hat on at all times and continue to be aware of the strategic decisions a startup makes over time. You may be an employee of the company, but you are the lead investor of your time and your career.

How to Think Like a Venture Capitalist: The Ten Factors You Need to Know When Evaluating Startups

5. How to Think Like a VC When Evaluating Startups:

All aspiring and current startup product managers have to think like venture capitalists. Let's explain more. As mentioned before, you need to keep your investor hat on when evaluating startups. You are investing at least a few months to a year at minimum of your career into a startup, the product, and the team. You are investing your energy and time into a startup. You need to gather as much information as possible when evaluating a startup. The table below covers the ten factors that you need to consider when analyzing startup opportunities.

The Startup Product Manager's Ten Factors to Evaluate	Questions to Ask
Revenue	What are the various revenue streams of the startup? Is revenue recurring? What is the annual recurring revenue (ARR) and monthly recurring revenue (MRR)? What has been the trajectory of revenues over time? What are the revenue growth rates?
Costs	What are the top costs for the business currently? How much is spent on employees, marketing, third-party software, etc? Are costs greater than revenues, and if so, by how much?
Profitability	Is the startup currently profitable? What is on the product roadmap currently to help achieve profitability?
Customers	Who are the target customers? If you were to segment them by demographic, vertical, etc, how would you segment your revenues by the types of customers you have?

	What are the switching costs of your customers? Do your customers have any negotiating power? Are there any other products on the market that they are considering? If B2B: how many customers are under contract right now? How much revenue does each customer generate? What level of non-monetary impact do the customers have on the company? If B2C: how many customers does the startup have? How many daily active users (DAU) and monthly active users (MAU)? What is the startup's current strategy to acquire and retain customers?
Competitors	Who are the key competitors right now? Are they successful? Have they raised venture money? Is there any consolidation happening amongst existing competitors? How difficult is it for new competitors to come into the market?
Market	What is the market size? What part of the total market is the startup targeting? What is the growth rate for this market?
Raising Money	When does the startup expect to raise money next? What is the current runway?
User Experience	Does the company currently measure the net promoter scores

	(NPS) of its product?
Growth	What is the lifetime value of a customer (LTV) – how much revenue can you generate as long as the startup has the customer? What is the cost of customer acquisition (CAC) – how much does it cost to get one customer on average? What is the LTV:CAC ratio? Does the startup have any plans to upsell customers?
North Star Metric	Does the startup currently have a north star metric? Can you see if the founders are able to convey a level of focus on how they plan to execute on their vision?

CHAPTER 8

THE MUST-KNOW DIFFERENCES BETWEEN BUILDING B2B AND CONSUMER STARTUPS

There are different types of startups, and one of the most important distinctions you can make in your career is deciding whether you want to join a B2B or B2C company as a startup product manager. Building B2B startups is very different from building B2C startups. If you were a startup operator before, you have probably considered whether you have wanted to build B2B products or consumer products. Maybe you are considering your first or second career in the startup world and want to understand the differences better. Product management, design, marketing, and other roles are very distinct depending on the business model, the type of product, and who the end user is. You may be a current or future founder who is reading this right now: you may have wondered whether it is best for you to start a B2B company or a consumer-focused company. Alternatively, you may be a current or future investor evaluating B2B and consumer companies on a daily basis. As a startup product manager, you will have a significantly different role if you join a B2B versus a consumer company.

We can break down both types of startups to help you understand key differences in building B2B software versus consumer software products.

B2B vs B2C Businesses

1. What is B2B? What is B2C?

Most startups fall into one of two buckets: 1) B2B or 2) B2C.

- B2B stands for business to business. B2B startups create products and services, where businesses are the core customers.
- B2C stands for business to consumer. B2C is also known as "consumer." Consumer startups create products and services, where individual people are the core customers.

At its core, B2B is focused on businesses creating products and services that can be sold to other businesses.

- For example, Salesforce is a CRM (customer-relationship management) software product that helps teams track communication and the relationship journey with their customers — and more.

B2C is focused on businesses creating products and services directly to consumers — you, your friends, your family, and more.

- As another example, <u>Robinhood</u> is a digital brokerage and trading platform that allows traders to buy securities, such as stocks and ETFs. It is primarily known as a consumer company, but it does have B2B components. It generates most of its revenue from <u>payment for order flow</u>.

How Customer Bases Differ Between B2B and B2C Startups

2. How Customer Bases Differ Between B2B and B2C companies

B2C startups often need thousands of customers, at a minimum, to find themselves in the realm of successful venture-backed startups. B2B startups, on the other hand, may need one or a few customers to find themselves in the realm of successful venture-backed startups. Why is this the case? B2C startups typically monetize individual consumers, and there can be limits to how much revenue you can generate in exchange for providing value to a customer.

Spotify is a great example of a B2C-driven business model. Spotify typically charges $9.99 per month for its premium version, which lets its users listen to unlimited music without ads. In order to generate $1 million in revenue per year, Spotify has to have at least 8,342 paid subscribers a year. Each of the 8,342 subscribers generates $9.99 per month, times 12 months, equals just over $1 million in revenue. Alternatively, B2B startups can have one or a few great customers in order to reach the same level of revenue. HubSpot is a great example of a B2B-driven business model. HubSpot charges $3,600 per month for its enterprise solution, which provides the full suite of marketing, sales, and customer success software. In order to generate $1 million in revenue per year, HubSpot has to have at least 278 enterprise customers a year. If HubSpot were a very early startup, they would have only needed one enterprise customer to generate $43,200 in revenue.

Further, in B2B, usage-based pricing models often play a role in helping companies scale with relatively few customers. Enterprise contracts can be built in a way that enterprise customers are charged by how much they engage with and use the product. This allows B2B startups to scale a lot more quickly, even if they have one or a few customers. Beyond a set subscription fee, there may be a usage-based fee that scales based on how much a customer is willing to use the product. In these cases, you may see early B2B startups that are venture-backed, have product-market fit, and only have one or a few customers.

The Secrets to Scaling B2B Startups

3. The Secrets to Scaling B2B Startups

In B2B, you need a few key customers to get a foothold in the market you are operating in. Getting your first customers in B2B is hard. And when you are scaling, the sales cycle is significantly longer in B2B than in B2C. It may take a few quarters or even years to sign a customer in B2B. In B2C, the sales cycle can be much quicker and time to market can be faster. Although the sales cycle in B2B is longer than B2C, the opportunity exists in signing long-term contracts with customers that allow B2B businesses to have greater longevity when working with customers. After you develop relationships and onboard these key customers, they can define the future of your company drastically. Every partnership that your company has with a customer is important early on. It can take only a few quality customers for a B2B startup to find product-market fit. As a startup continues to find more quality customers, this may lead to a path to profitability after the company has found its product-market fit.

The company can then scale into growth mode. Once a B2B company is in growth mode, if the operators make the right decisions, the company can be on a path to continued success that will compound over time. It is important to note that six customers will not guarantee that your company will succeed or dominate a market. However, it does set the stage for your startup to find more customers and for you to continue planning for future growth. It allows your marketing and sales teams to pitch the product and services you are selling more effectively to new customers because it has already been validated by your existing customers. It gives your product, design, and engineering teams a greater purpose to keep going because they are solving problems for these core customers — and helping them succeed.

As a startup product manager, you will recognize that your outcomes early on will depend heavily on identifying opportunities to help your initial customer base succeed. Your ability to solve problems for these few customers is critical, and it partially plays into how the startup will get more customers. B2B customers may either directly or indirectly influence a product roadmap. It is ultimately up to the product team and the startup's discretion to determine how much these B2B customers can influence the roadmap. Startup product managers at B2B startups need to balance their time building to solve problems for their core customers with solving the greatest problems in the market for all potential customers. There may be overlap between the opportunities to help current customers and the opportunities to help all potential customers in the broader market. It is important to create the best experience for these initial customers, while strategizing on a roadmap that is flexible enough to address broader needs in the market to acquire additional customers.

Industry experience is critical for the founding team to have in order to succeed in most B2B environments. Most commonly, you will see founders who have worked either in that space directly or an adjacent area prior to founding the company. These founders have developed a unique lens into the market they are operating in and have had skin in the game. This gives them the opportunity to develop a vision around how they want to solve problems in the space and can have thoughtful conversations with customers early on. Having industry experience (ex: financial services, healthcare, etc) beyond functional expertise (product management, design, marketing, customer success) is the greatest challenge for scaling in B2B. That also makes it an exciting opportunity for operators because you learn about new industries quickly and gain functional expertise rapidly. Startup product managers particularly excel in B2B startups when they come in with previous industry experience or if they transition from another role. Having knowledge of the industry and market you are operating in builds up your ability to identify problems to solve and prioritize opportunities for your team.

The Secrets to Scaling Consumer Startups

4. The Secrets to Scaling Consumer Startups

When building consumer products, you need traction. You start out with a few users initially, and it is your job to retain a consistent daily and monthly user base that engages with the product. Your users need to grow to hundreds, eventually thousands, maybe even millions (or billions) of users. You need a supportive army of people that use your product and are customers that you retain over time. Consumer software needs to be prioritized differently in terms of the features you build. Quicker onboarding flows are a necessity and features that keep users on the platform are crucial because user metrics are important; it needs to be a highly responsive product that you use on your phone, your personal computer, tablet, and more. For consumer software, metrics and data have to play a greater role early on. Every software product you build is in part a lead generation tool for your business. You need to track the dropoff at every stage of the process. Feature conversion and conversion tracking are also key principles of growing consumer products. Stickiness is important both in growing B2B and Consumer products. You will need to develop strategies to monetize your user base in order to generate revenue. This can be a bit different than B2B since users for consumer products are often not bound to long-term contractual agreements. There are more differences between B2B and consumer products that we will cover in the next section.

Must-Know Differences Between B2B and B2C Startups

5. B2B vs B2C: Customer Growth & Retention, Prioritization, and Relatability

Consumer startups present their own exciting challenges. In B2B, you should aim to keep all of your customers happy. The earlier a B2B startup is, the more influence each individual customer has. Consumer startups frankly may not know every single customer they have early on, but they still need to build the best experience to make them love using the product. Customers can have more influence in B2B: the core problems they have **need** to be addressed. In B2B, you have agreed to deliver on your contractual agreements with your customers. You will have a working partnership for at least a few months to many months (or years). Given that B2B startups have a few core customers early on, it is imperative that you try your best to keep them all happy. They are the ones who will vouch for you when you are looking for more customers or raising your next round. You will often communicate with most customers directly in B2B, while in B2C it is less common that you will (because there are so many customers). Retaining a customer in B2B versus in consumer can have more weight and impact. For consumer startups, it is much more challenging to address every customer problem and customer request as you scale. You will need to ruthlessly prioritize particular user groups. Prioritizing at consumer startups differs from prioritizing at B2B startups. In B2B, you already know who your direct customers are so you likely will build based on the problems they have that you identify and prioritize solutions for them. You still cannot solve every single need or issue for them, so you will need to ruthlessly prioritize in B2B as well. In consumer startups, you have more leverage as a startup product manager in deciding what to prioritize. At B2B startups, you will be influenced directly by your customers: they have a seat at the table. It is your job to communicate and decide whether you will address a request from them. Early on, you need to learn how to effectively communicate with your customers and create channels for communication with them at B2B startups. The problems you solve for your initial customers set the foundation for your product team. You can additionally build for problems that you see existing beyond this group of core customers, but it needs to have a balance with your current paying customers. The balance you need in B2B is growing current revenue streams through existing product lines that address the needs of your current customers, while optimizing for creative features for newly found problems for current and future customers.

Building consumer products differs from building B2B products from a relatability standpoint. Building for everyday consumers is different from building for enterprise businesses. Consumer products are naturally more tangible and relatable. They may be products you could see yourself, your friends, and your family using (depending on the goal of the product). Product managers and designers may directly empathize with the end product and user. The more effectively you can understand your end user, the better you can create solutions for them. For designers, this is a very important distinction because you would conduct user research, brainstorm solutions, and design prototypes. Knowing your preference for B2B or consumer products is important here. Even if a product is not as relatable, it presents its own exciting opportunities and challenges for operators.

Another important distinction to make involves knowing that all of the features of a B2B product are not universally used by a single user. Certain features are built out for specific use cases for different types of users. Consumer product teams may opt for depth when building features for one type of target user, while

B2B product teams may go for breadth when building features for multiple types of target users. It is also important to note that product managers who build a B2B product may not be a direct user of all features of the product. For example, you may be a startup product manager who is working on software for a corporate card that small and medium businesses would use. If you do not own a small and medium business, you may not directly use **all** of the features of the product. You still have to understand how these consumers use your product. Alternatively, you could be working on an ads platform for a major social media company. You may understand how everyday consumers interact with the ads they see, but it may be difficult to understand how businesses interact with the ads platform if you have never owned a business or created paid ads targeted for businesses.

B2B is especially complex because it is multi-faceted with the types of users. The customer segments can be much more complex. One B2B customer may be significantly different than another B2B customer. They could be at different stages of growth, have different problems, be different size companies in terms of employees, sell different products, operate in different markets, and more. It makes it more complex to serve all of these needs early on as a startup. It also makes it more challenging for a startup product manager to understand every customer. If you are at an early stage startup, the breadth of features that you will manage will be significantly greater than it would be at a big tech company. Product managers at B2B and consumer startups take on broader responsibilities than they would at traditional tech companies. You would be in charge of leading multiple parts of the product, and the closer you are in communication with the founders and core customers, the more likely you are to take on senior level responsibilities. At an early startup, you are more likely a "VP of Product" than a "Product Manager" due to the responsibilities you take on. Joining an early stage startup as a product manager will catapult you into the action. Your responsibilities will be much greater than what may initially be considered as a more junior product management role. Given that your responsibilities will be so broad, especially at a B2B company where the products are typically more complex than consumer products, it is critical that you try to understand your product and your customers deeply. There are certain features you may never fully understand. However, you must try your best to understand the following: *who uses the product, why do they use it, and how do they use it?* When building a B2B product, you may never fully understand every single use case that exists for your customers. There will be stakeholders who come in with their own ideas. Focus is particularly important for B2B companies because there are so many customers who you can design solutions for. You have to find a balance between understanding every customer and every part of the product. You are constantly challenged to think outside of the box. Prioritization in B2B is what differentiates good startup product managers from great startup product managers.

A notable difference between building B2B products and consumer products is the level of focus on funnel metrics early on, specifically around acquisition, conversion, and retention of customers. Consumer products require experimentation, testing, and validation to find the feature or product that works well. You are consistently tracking funnel metrics. Conversion rates, drop off rates, and user growth rates are all important in your day to day work as a startup product manager at a consumer company. Metrics such as daily active users (DAU) and monthly active users (MAU) are typically more relevant for consumer teams. You also need to track the conversion rate of customers from one stage to the next and end to end conversion. You can further conduct A/B tests to see how you can improve drop off. In terms of the number of customers you have, there is greater fluctuation typically in user counts at consumer startups versus B2B startups. You may gain (or lose) a hundred customers in a day for a fast-growing consumer product, but that is almost unheard of at B2B startups. Certain user metrics are not used as often at B2B companies because it is typically well-known across the company when new customers are signed or when a customer leaves. At B2B startups, when the company partners with a new customer, these are pivotal moments and big events early on because every new customer has a drastic impact in moving the needle forward. At consumer startups, it is more about compounding growth. When you can continue to grow your customer base from hundreds, to thousands, to millions, you begin to experience different levels of product-market fit. The quantity of customers is critical in growing consumer products early on. The quantity of quality customers is critical across both consumer and B2B startups.

In the end, B2B and consumer software products are similarly built from a functionality standpoint: at a fundamental level, the design and engineering skills required are relatively similar. The differences exist in *what* you build and *how* you think about building it. The core differentiator in building B2B versus consumer products is that you are building within different contexts. The context in which a designer executes or an engineer executes is important. The more relevant context and information they have around the problem they are solving for, the more effectively they can build a product that solves that problem. Several factors are contextually different when building B2B and consumer products: the types of end users, growth strategies, user retention strategies, prioritization of problems, stakeholder management, the types of metrics, and more. Knowing the differences between B2B and consumer startups can help you be a better builder, operator, and investor.

Ultimately, you should try to understand whether building B2B companies or building consumer companies is right for you. B2B companies, on average, are easier to raise funding for and are viewed as easier to scale. You only need a few large customers to succeed. Consumer startups may require thousands or millions of customers to succeed. You should also be conscious of how a consumer startup could expand to include a B2B business model and ask those questions to the founders.

"Largely true: first time founders start consumer companies. Second time founders start B2B companies." – Elizabeth Yin

However, you may find that your interests and skill sets as a startup product manager better suit building consumer products over B2B products. If this is the case, you may discover that scaling consumer products is easier. Even if B2B products seem easier to scale on the outside, you will never know until you experience building both types of products. In order to find yourself doing your best work as a startup product manager, you need to find startups that play to your strengths, skill sets, and interests.

To understand the best startup fit for you, you need to try building both types of products. This comes with time and experience. If you are a new or aspiring startup product manager, you need to begin developing a diverse set of skills and be able to pitch your background to founders. We will go over practical ways you can build core skills to help launch your career on the right trajectory.

CHAPTER 9

WHY LEARNING TO DESIGN AND CODE ARE SUPERPOWERS FOR STARTUP PRODUCT MANAGERS

No, learning to design and code are not necessary at all to become a startup product manager. I want to dispel any notion that you **need** to learn how to design or code. **However, trust me: do not skip this chapter.** Yes, you will likely never directly design or write code as a startup product manager. Once in a while, you may edit a Figma file here or there and write a few lines of HTML. At an early stage startup, your main job is to define what to build and prioritize the important pieces of the vision. You then have to trust the right people to help you execute on that vision, and they will determine exactly how to build it. However, in order to effectively define what to build and prioritize effectively, you should grow your background in design and programming. I often hear that you need to learn these skills *before* you become a startup product manager, and this is a valid point of view. But not everyone has the same journey. You do not need these skills from day one. You can always continue to learn design and programming on the side regardless of whether you land a startup product manager role or not, through building projects or taking courses. You also do not need to be a superstar either, but I highly recommend that you try. You should **try** to learn and apply the design process through case studies or side projects. You should **try** to learn how to code and build side projects. Later, I will focus on practical ways **how** you can learn to design and code. First, I want to focus on **why** learning to design and code are valuable for new or aspiring product managers. These lessons are particularly drawn from my experiences as a startup product manager.

Learning to design and code will help you empathize with your teams better. Learning to design and code will help you prioritize initiatives better. You will be able to think more strategically about what to build. On top of this, as you continue to grow your business judgment, you will be able to identify opportunities for a startup that will move the needle forward. All of these skills will compound your career growth. Startup product management is about connective thinking: you are combining your experiences to solve problems for customers and build a better business. You need to draw from your superpowers and channel this energy into deciding what to build. Startup product managers have to make strategic decisions and lay the groundwork for proper execution. In order to become great at both, you have to build and invest in your talent roadmap. With a well-rounded skill set, it will accelerate your growth as a startup product manager. If you learn how to design and code, you are learning **how** to build. If you learn how to build, you will instinctively become the best startup product manager you can be.

"I believe that product instincts can be trained, especially when you develop from a foundation of strength." – Linda Zhang

https://www.productlessons.xyz/article/how-to-develop-talent-stack

The Most Important Investment: Your Talent Roadmap

1. Startup product managers can become more well-rounded by focusing on their talent roadmap. By doing so, they can become a top 1% startup product manager.

You should view your career as an ever-evolving product. Startup product managers need to have a talent roadmap that they consistently execute on, either formally or informally. You are essentially the main character in a video game where you are constantly growing your various skills. New or aspiring startup product managers, early on, should focus on growing their fundamental knowledge about designing and developing products. Strategizing and executing on your talent roadmap is an enormous investment you can make in your startup product management career. The earlier you are in your career, you need to taste and sample multiple fields. Aim to be a generalist as long as you can. You focus on a few core areas instead of going deep in one area. It is a continuous journey of improvement, and when you discover the area you want to go deep in, you can always focus more there. Everyone is capable of furthering their skill sets and becoming a successful startup product manager. Now, you are probably wondering: what are the exact skills I need to develop? We will cover that now.

Linda Zhang, a product manager who helped scale a Series A startup that is now a decacorn, wrote an amazing blog post for product managers. Here are a few important insights from Linda Zhang's blog post: "How to develop your talent stack."

- *"Develop a variety of skills that make you unique."*
- *"You don't need to be the top 1% to be in the top 1%. By crafting a unique concoction of useful skills, you enter a league of your own."*
- *"If you already spike on one of the skills [below], pursuing the other half will pay dividends. And when you triple up, you'll run circles. By becoming more interdisciplinary, you position yourself to connect the dots invisible to others."*

"The skills that are most paradoxical and rarely found in the same person include: 1) Design instincts x business principles, 2) Design instincts x data analysis, 3) Storytelling x coding, 4) Storytelling x data analysis, 5) Business principles x coding." – Linda Zhang.
https://www.productlessons.xyz/article/
how-to-develop-talent-stack

The five core skills a startup product manager can develop are similar to the ones mentioned above. This is not an exhaustive list of questions or skills to ask yourself. It is a great foundation:

Startup Product Manager Core Skills	Questions to Ask Yourself
Design	Have you conducted user research and usability tests? Do you have knowledge of design principles? Do you understand the stages of the double-diamond design process? Have you applied design principles? How comfortable are you with user experience design versus visual design? Have you redesigned products, critiqued products, worked on side projects, or built case studies?
Business	Have you built a business? Have you failed in building a business, and if so, what have you learned? Have you succeeded in building a business? Have you worked with customers? Do you understand strategy versus execution? How have you handled conflict or competition? Have you managed people? Are you comfortable relating business metrics to product metrics?
Communication	How comfortable are you with stakeholder management? Are you able to tell stories to your teams? Do you frequently share context with team members? Have you worked cross-functionally with different teams? Have you been able to speak the language of several different teams? Can you delegate? Have you been able to encourage or empower team members before? Can you manage up? Are you strong in written communication? Are you strong in spoken communication?

Coding	Do you have working knowledge of the foundations of backend and frontend languages? Have you taken programming courses or went to a coding bootcamp? Have you built side projects before? Have you worked with other engineers before? Have you iterated on a project before and updated it based on feedback? Have you solved bugs before?
Data	Have you used metrics before to assist in your decision making? Have you worked with product metrics before (active user counts, adoption, engagement, retention, etc)? Have you performed A/B tests? Have you tested hypotheses before and validated them through data? If you needed to analyze data before, have you created reports using software or worked with individuals to analyze data?

If you can get a combination of two or more of these skills and learn these skills well enough, you will become a top 1% startup product manager. Most people hone in on one skill and do that well. In order to set yourself apart, however, you should have a basket of skills and become a generalist. Many product managers do not have a combination of these skills, but the ones who stand out and succeed are able to grasp and grow in multiple fields. You need to invest in leveling up your skills and be obsessed with the journey. The goal here is not to learn every skill, but the goal here is to be able utilize these skills to make better strategic product decisions, keep your team members informed, and empower those who you work with to execute. The benefit of working at a startup is that you are often encouraged to develop multiple skills. The earlier you can determine what your strengths are and which skills you want to develop, the quicker your career growth will compound. The more you invest into multiple skills, the more effective you will be on the job.

As a startup product manager, you need to learn how to build. In this chapter, the two core "building" skills I want to help you further develop are design and coding. First, we will go over higher-level strategies and later dive deeper into the nuances of building your design and coding skills.

The best way to learn how to "build" is by doing. These are two methods that helped me learn how to build:

- **Working on side projects**: through side projects, you get to choose what you want to learn. This is lower risk and can be done in your free time. You can be anyone: a student, a full-time employee, etc. After classes, after work, or during any break, you can build and create side projects. These projects give you hands-on skills and teach you how to build a better startup product management mindset.
- **Joining a startup**: this is the quickest way to learn multiple skills. This can be a full-time or part-time job. As a startup product manager full-time, you will directly learn about these skills because you will interact with different teams

on a daily basis. I would recommend working on side projects if your schedule permits as mentioned before. If you are a student, you may have time to explore part-time roles in other product-adjacent roles: design, marketing, coding, etc. These can be virtual opportunities that you take during the year before a traditional summer internship. When looking for full-time opportunities, you can always start out in a product-adjacent role and then transition into product management as well.

Now, we will focus on how to specifically learn how to design and code in practical ways through step-by-step actions.

The Secret to Learning Product Design: A Step-by-Step Strategy

2. The most effective way to learn design is by doing, here is how to start and succeed:

Design is an end to end process. The double-diamond design process is the most common approach that product designers take today when designing. The double-diamond design process involves understanding customer problems, defining the problem you want to focus on, testing various solutions to the problem with customers, and iterating on the primary solution you hope to move forward with. Of course, in practice, it is modified at startups and big tech companies. As a startup product manager, you should actively learn about the design process. You should try to solve an existing problem that exists in the world and create a case study on it.

The double-diamond design process involves two phases: the research phase and the design phase.

- **In the research phase**, it is important to deeply understand the problem. You focus on problem discovery and defining the scope of the problem you are solving. As soon as you begin to define the problem, you move onto the design phase.

- **In the design phase**, it is critical to begin thinking about solutions for the problem you defined. You brainstorm and test various solutions. Design is about iteration. Your solutions are received with feedback from customers, and you begin to prioritize the highest impact solutions through testing on customers. It is important to understand and have a balance between impact and feasibility for engineering when they begin to implement these designs. We will talk more about prioritization in an upcoming chapter.

  Source:

  https://en.wikipedia.org/wiki/Double_Diamond_(design_proce ss_model)

In short, you learn about design by being problem and customer focused. If you want to be the **best** startup product manager you can be, you should train to become a product designer first.

Practical Strategies to Learning The Design Process

3. There are practical ways to learn about the design process:

- Take a Digital Product Design or Human-Computer Interaction Design course at your local university. If you enjoyed the course after taking it, you can also potentially become a teaching assistant for the course and help mentor students as well! Even if you are not a student, you can find other programs that are available to those who have graduated or for full-time professionals.
  - Digital Product Design Course Example: https://www.cornellappdev.com/courses/dpd
  - Human-Computer Interaction Design Course: https://classes.cornell.edu/browse/roster/SP22/class/INFO/3450
- Explore Google's UX Design Certificate Program:
  - Google's UX Design Certificate Program: https://grow.google/certificates/ux-design/#?modal_active=none

- Consider a Design Bootcamp. Aim for the longer programs (minimum 4 weeks) to receive a deeper understanding of the process. There are multiple design bootcamps you can choose from, as seen below.

  o The factors to consider when looking at bootcamps can involve the following: the cost of the bootcamp, length of the bootcamp, goals of the bootcamp, and projects from the bootcamp. The learnings and tangible projects you get from a design bootcamp are critical. A case study can help you promote yourself: it can become a portfolio piece you can then use to pitch to startups and serve as a quick way to demonstrate your multi-faceted product skills.

Bootcamp Name	Website
General Assembly	https://generalassemb.ly/education/user-experience-design/new-york-city
CareerFoundry	https://careerfoundry.com/en/courses/become-a-ux-designer/
Springboard	https://www.springboard.com/courses/ui-ux-design-career-track/
Flatiron School	https://flatironschool.com/courses/product-design-bootcamp/

Thinkful	https://www.thinkful.com/bootcamp/ux-ui/
Avocademy	https://www.avocademy.com/
Ironhack	https://www.ironhack.com/en/ux-ui-design
DesignLab	https://designlab.com/
Memorisely	https://www.memorisely.com/live-bootcamp/ux-ui-bootcamps/ux-ui-design-bootcamp
Mento Design Academy	https://www.mentodesign.academy/

- o Here is a video on choosing a UX Design Bootcamp: Which UX Bootcamp is the Best? Why I Chose Springboard 🖤(General Assembly, CareerFoundry)

Through a design bootcamp, you will solidify your understanding of the design process and apply your learnings in practical ways to create a foundation for the rest of your career as a product manager. The design process is comprehensive. You can learn about defining problem spaces, writing problem statements, conducting user research, prioritizing solutions, creating personas, designing low/mid/high fidelity prototypes, brainstorming, identifying solution spaces, conducting SWOT analyses, conducting market research, doing usability testing, creating an information hierarchy, making a design system, and more.

How to Create a Design Case Study

4. How to Create a Design Case Study (Bootcamp Secrets):

Throughout a course or bootcamp, you can create a design case study. Creating a design case study is a visualized version of the double-diamond design process referenced earlier. Creating a case study helps you understand design and become a product thinker.

Here is an example of a case study that I created. This is purely educational to help you build one without a bootcamp or to even supplement what you learn in a bootcamp. It became a core part of my portfolio and helped me land product management roles. Feel free to use it as inspiration and a reference for when you build your own case study:

- *"Case study: how to revolutionize investing through financial education and community" (https://bootcamp.uxdesign.cc/a-new-way-to-learn-robinhood-case-study-2f9df0fa1868)*

Learning design through a case study helps you develop product sense: design is at the intersection of psychology and problem-solving. This makes it fun and fulfilling. Product sense is a skill that can be learned, grown, and honed. Product sense is your ability to anticipate customer needs, prioritize problems to solve for, and create effective solutions to customer problems. You need to have a deep understanding of your customers, while being able to channel your inner creativity to create effective solutions. Note: the way you think is important, in terms of how you bring an open mind to approaching problems and forming solutions. The solution itself does not have to be creative: it can be a simple or complex solution that solves a problem.

The skills you learn through creating a design case study are absolutely useful as a startup product manager. I will give you the step-by-step guide on how to create a design case study below that involves a re-design of an existing mobile app.

How to create a design case study (higher-level overview):

1. **Problem discovery:** you choose a market and broad audience within that space that you want to learn more about. You begin to identify people you want to interview. They do not have to be existing customers or users of a particular product. You begin to interview them and understand their problems through user research. You ask questions about **how** they do things and engage in activities. In this stage, you identify pain points they have in these processes.

Understanding How and Why People Invest on Robinhood

After conducting a few interviews with friends and peers, I asked them more about their experiences choosing investments on Robinhood. Here is what I learned:

1. Robinhood makes it easy to invest — but people didn't do much in-depth analysis of investments, and Robinhood does not encourage learning as much as it should

"Robinhood encourages "brainless investing" — i.e) "look at the chart and just invest, without doing any research on the company."

I have just been "learning the mindset of "buy low, sell high."

I "never had a formal education before using Robinhood."

2. **Persona creation and problem definition:** you recognize and establish the different personas you find that make up the audience in this market. There may be two or more personas you can create. You begin to create a list of problems and common themes you are seeing amongst these personas. You prioritize and define the problem you are interested in solving for. From your initial interviews, you may intuitively know which problem interests you the most. Alternatively, you can prioritize the problem you want to solve by the potential impact and feasibility of solving the problem.

The New Investor

C

Charles
College Student

Goals
· Learning the basics of investing
· Talking to friends about stocks

Pain Points / Issues
· Not knowing where to start or look
· Trouble picking stocks, not sure what a good strategy is

The Experienced Investor

S

Samantha
College Student

Goals
· Learning more nuanced fundamentals of investing
· Reading what the experts are saying, talking to other experts

Pain Points / Issues
· Discovering good analysis on investments is hard
· Always has to look outside of Robinhood to learn more about her investments

3. Formation of the problem statement: you should create a clear problem statement and then provide two to three bullet points why this is a problem.

How I Arrived at This Point

People Problem: When I am considering investing in a company as an average investor ("retail investor"), I want to understand the basics of various investing strategies, so that I can evaluate whether it is logical to invest in a stock or not for the future. But I can't do that well because...

1. It's hard to find resources on investing, buzzwords, and finance fundamentals that are written in plain English as well as easily understandable by anyone.

2. It's tedious to find a list of investment strategies that are already backed by experts.

3. I want a community of people that I can learn from by interacting and participating with them

4. **Brainstorming Solutions:** at this stage, you want to begin brainstorming solutions with individuals who are within the target audience you are solving for. You should pick two or more individuals who you can have a brainstorming session with using Miro, Figma, etc. At the start, you present the problem statement you formed earlier. Each person creates 20 ideas for how they would solve the problem you had. After this, you would categorize the ideas into solution spaces. You are essentially creating an affinity diagram and categorizing the ideas by similarity. After this, you choose the six solution spaces you are most interested in. From there, your team should vote on the three that you are most excited about solving for and present the most potential. The solution spaces you vote on the most are the core opportunity areas for designing out tangible solutions. After this stage, you begin to create designs to solve the problem you defined earlier.

Initial Brainstorming

To start, I recruited a few friends, Andres and Gonzalo, to virtually brainstorm with me on Miro. From a few hundred post-its, we ideated ways that would allow users to **learn** and have a social experience through **community.**

Our brainstorming led to three opportunity areas: "learning specific, personalized learning, and community." Within these three opportunity areas, we narrowed our ideas into **three solution spaces.**

1. **Strategies, basics of personal finance/markets, articles + Tutorials:** we saw a lot of overlap between two of the solution spaces and decided to consider them collectively as one. We felt that learning about investing as well as some of the foundational knowledge may help provide context for potential investments, giving people more factors to consider when making an investment.

2. **Community Outreach**: This idea of community is one that people desire, and having people interact with one another would provide a social aspect to investments, which currently can be an isolated activity.

3. **Competition:** may lead to pe 👏 82 ◯ ompete with one another to make better investments in general and be able to allow those who are

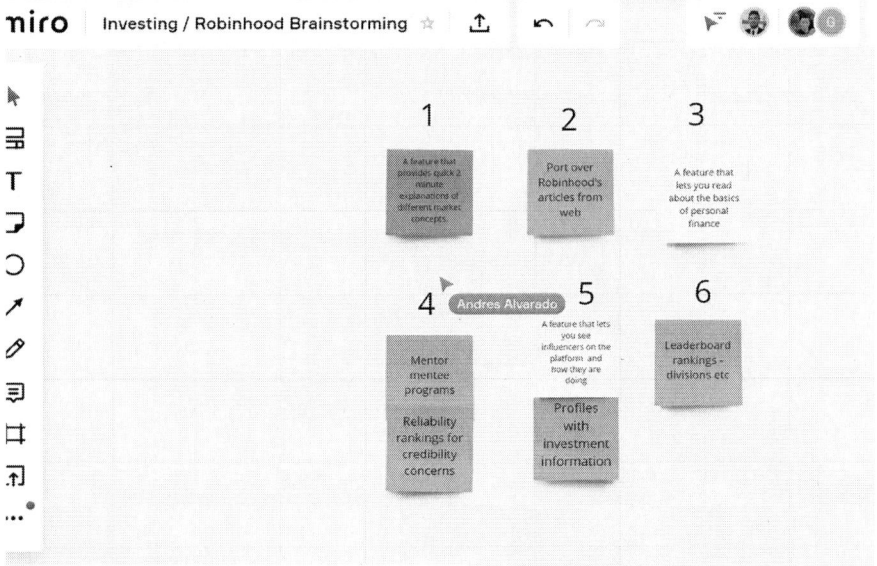

5. **Sketching Low-Fidelity Designs:** now, you should design out your initial approach to the problem. This can be a sketch with pen and paper. You need to design the change you want to see to the existing flow. The updated flow should involve a new user experience that addresses the problem statement you defined earlier. This is the low-fidelity prototype, which will then be updated and iterated on through your medium-fidelity and high-fidelity prototypes.

Initial Approach

As noted below, I wanted to focus on the initial sketches (low-fidelity) for the feature.

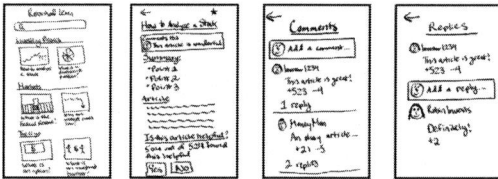
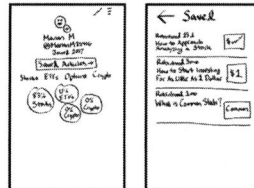

6. **SWOT Analysis**: You should create a SWOT analysis of the strengths, weaknesses, opportunities, and threats for your current product. You should evaluate the product and company as a whole in your SWOT analysis.

Strengths

- Robinhood has resources on its website, can be ported onto app

- Provides an ecosystem of resources to build off of

- Simple and easy to understand, has visuals

Weaknesses

- Articles can be very/broad vague in nature

- Articles are not all-encompassing, it doesn't present necessarily the most up-to-date information

- Theory presented in articles doesn't always translate to practicality/success in investing

Opportunities

- Supplementing Robinhood articles with the podcast (Robinhood Snacks) as resources

- Users can vote on how helpful the article is to vet the article for credibility purposes

- Users with built-up credibility can start publishing posts if they would like to. Also interaction via comments system & community

- Might be helpful to show how these articles have helped users succeed on Robinhood (testimonies)

- Creating structured categories for types of articles i.e) markets, finance fundamentals, etc

Threats

- too much information (if unorganized) may confuse users and potentially lead them to leave the app

- contributors can be poached to other apps/companies and not post on Robinhood anymore

7. Market Research and Competitive Analysis: You need to conduct research on a few of the core products and services that relate to your solution. The solution chosen for this example was around community and education, so it prompted a review of other products out there that had similar solutions. The goal is to create your own solution, which is the best solution for your product and customers.

   a. Check it out here: *"Case study: how to revolutionize investing through financial education and community" (https://bootcamp.uxdesign.cc/a-new-way-to-learn-robinhood-case-study-2f9df0fa1868)*

8. **Information hierarchy**: you should define the hierarchy of the structure of the product you are working on, and any new features should be included as well.

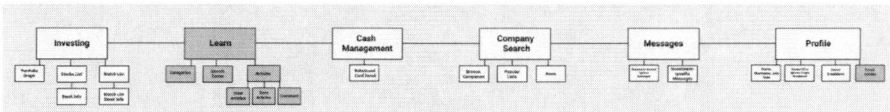

9. **Creating Medium-Fidelity Designs:** based on the SWOT analysis and market research you conducted, you can begin to design out the future flow in more detail. If you are redesigning a mobile app, you can recreate the components of the screens you will redesign. If you are creating an entirely new product, you can begin to visually form your experience and aesthetic: how users will interact with it, how the experience is meaningful to them, and how your visual design will be formed. You should have multiple explorations and design the ways a user can interact with your new flow. The explorations begin at the entry points of where users begin to interact with the new experience. The medium-fidelity prototype is the foundation you begin to lay for your usability testing and high-fidelity prototypes.

Exploration 1:

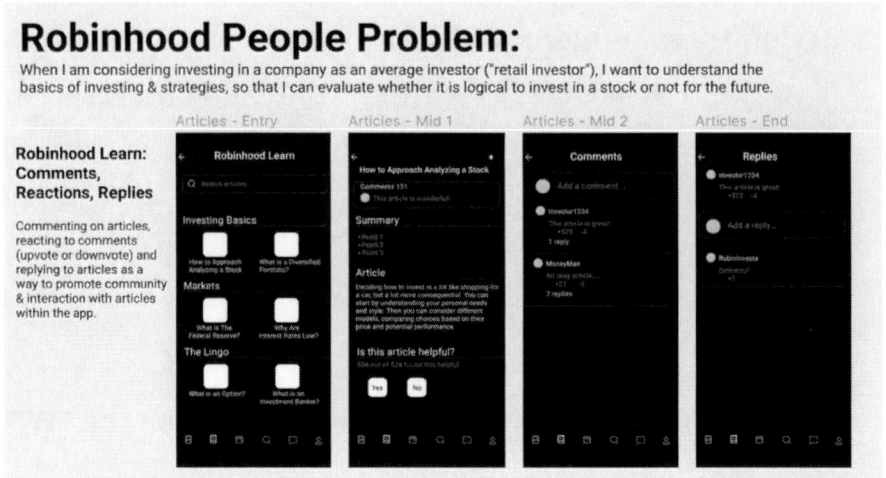

Robinhood People Problem:
When I am considering investing in a company as an average investor ("retail investor"), I want to understand the basics of investing & strategies, so that I can evaluate whether it is logical to invest in a stock or not for the future.

Exploration #1 — has the main article page as the entry point because this serves as the initial screen where the main feature is located. This entry point

10. **Usability Testing:** at this point, you will have a prototype that you can conduct usability tests on with your target audience. You will set the context, ask them to complete tasks, and observe how they complete tasks. The tasks are geared towards evaluating if your solution solves the problem you defined. Now, it will not be perfect. Using the feedback and observations you make during this stage, you can use this to form your high-fidelity prototype.

11. **Finalizing your high-fidelity prototype:** you would use the feedback that you gathered from your usability tests to finalize your high-fidelity prototype. The user experience will change, and your visual design will begin to reflect your

vision. You can also create a video and animate your prototype, as well as show how it can be an actual product.

The Fun Part — High Fidelity Prototyping!

Final Interaction for Robinhood Learn:

I added in vertical scrolling for the article (as seen in the beginning), more pictures, and prompted changes based on user feedback.

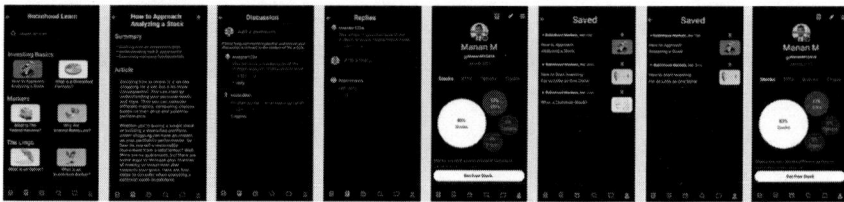

https://www.youtube.com/watch?v=JMFvXnDefhY&

12. **Creating a design system (optional):** You can create a design system for your product. There were a few assumptions made here and estimates on the colors, as well as fonts. The purpose of this is to serve as an educational resource for you in creating a design system. A design system includes the components, colors, and standards for your product. This is particularly important if you are creating a new product, and the design system can be something you use in the future if you ever revisit this case study in the future. You can create a tangible product from your prototypes.

Visual Design System for Robinhood:

This is primarily the existing design system for Robinhood that I was able to create for Android.

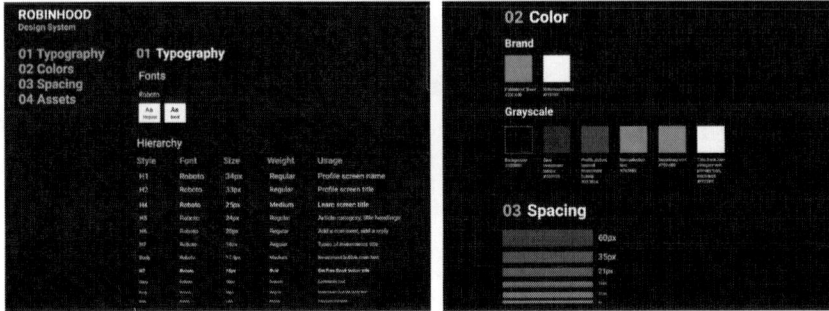

In reality, these are not all of the stages you will directly engage in as a startup product manager. Developing a product, in practice, is much different than this. It depends on the needs of your customers and startup. However, this gives you empathy and a deep understanding of your designers. Designers are your direct partners. The better working chemistry a startup product manager and designer have, the significantly better the product you ship will be.

My advice to aspiring and current startup product managers is to always consider creating a design case study! If you enjoy psychology, human behavior, and problem-solving, or are just curious about design, this is a highly recommended step to explore. This is not only a fun process but also an intensive process. You learn a lot by creating a case study, whether it is redesigning an existing app or creating a new product. Understanding how to solve problems, studying what makes a great user experience, practicing visual design, and more are all highly practical skills that you can carry with you throughout your career. Whether you stay as a product manager (or become a founder, investor, or anything else), you should know how to identify great design and how to empower people to execute. This is the secret.

Why a Design Case Study Will Help You Land a PM Role (And Become a Great PM!)

5. Why Creating a Design Case Study Will Help You Stand Out

A case study can be a **huge** differentiator that will help you stand out as an up-and-coming startup product manager. When you cold email founders or try to get your foot in the door, you can have a portfolio of side projects that you have built and use it to demonstrate your design skills. I have met very few product managers who have had a design background. A design case study will help you land your startup product manager role because it will make you stand out during interviews, as well as on the job. It also builds your product thinking abilities when it comes to discovery, problem definition, brainstorming, and prioritization. A case study helped me land a full-time startup product manager role and receive recognition from Lewis C. Lin.

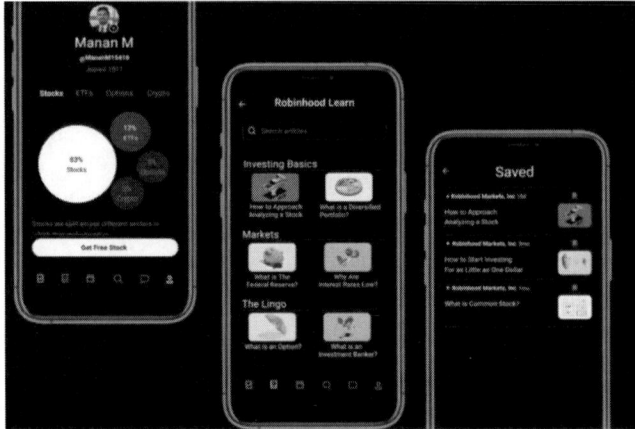

Lewis C. Lin • 1st
8x Bestselling Author | CEO x 2 | Follow for PM insig...
1yr •

An excellent example of what a PM portfolio piece should look like from **Manan Modi**

#productmanagement

Case study: how to revolutionize Investing through financial education and community

medium.com • 1 min read

You and 91 others   4 comments

https://www.linkedin.com/posts/lewislin_case-study-how-to-revolutionize-investing-activity-6759505820184137728-e2a1/

More importantly, it creates the foundation for you to work with designers and empathize with their process. The Product Manager and Designer dynamic is one of the most important partnerships. You need to be able to understand and work well with your designers. And if you enjoy design, it will come naturally to you with time. Your curiosity will help you collaborate better with your design team!

The Secret to Learning How to Code as a PM – And How it Will Help You Build Your PM Brand

6. How to learn how to code and build your brand as a product manager successfully:

The one project I recommend to anyone who is looking to learn how to code is a personal website. A personal website primarily uses frontend languages: HTML, CSS, and JS. I took a web design and development course, though there are many free resources available online to make a great personal website. All of this knowledge to build a website online is freely available.

- Course Reference:
  https://classes.cornell.edu/browse/roster/FA21/class/INFO/1300

- Free Course: HTML CSS and Javascript Website Design Tutorial - Beginner Project Fully Responsive by Brian Design

Also, there are several free courses on backend development if that interests you as well (Harvard CS50).

- Free introductory course from Harvard:
  https://pll.harvard.edu/course/cs50-introduction-computer-science?delta=0

However, I highly advise you to build a personal website as your first project if your goal is to become a product manager. It will help you understand the effort it takes to build a project, and given a website is primarily constructed through frontend languages, you will be able to visually identify every change. I recommend a personal website for a few more reasons: it will help you understand product design, you will actively consider tradeoffs for your website, it will help create a personal brand for you, and it provides long-term value while being less time consuming than other projects. When you create a personal website, you can be the product manager, developer, and designer all at once.

Resources to use for building a website:

- W3 Schools (helps you learn the basics of HTML/CSS/JS): https://www.w3schools.com/
- CodePen (provides inspiration for building frontend components): https://codepen.io/search/pens
- Stack Overflow (assists you if you have any questions or blockers when coding): https://stackoverflow.com/
- GitHub Pages (provides free website hosting): Host a website using GitHub Pages #Shorts
- Namecheap or Google Domains (sells cheap domain names)

Building a website helps you understand what goes into the basics of a development process. It will allow you to have better judgment when working with developers. You will learn how short or long it takes to build a feature. Velocity depends from developer to developer, but you will begin to understand what may take two weeks versus two months. Startup product managers should have some form of a technical understanding because you will interface with developers constantly. If you want to go beyond creating a personal website, you can work on learning other languages such as Python.

Creating a personal website also helps you market yourself better as a product manager. Especially for new or aspiring product managers, a personal website allows you to "pitch" yourself. It is also impressive to see when a product manager puts in the time and effort to learn how to code. And as mentioned before, when you develop your talent stack, you can have multiple skills beyond coding. If you combine a personal website with a design case study, along with a set of experiences on your resume that highlight your personal impact in a quantified way, you will have a convincing pitch and argument. The better the story you can craft for your career, the more persuasive you will be in your efforts to land a role. It will also make you a better product manager and pay dividends for your career. The more well-rounded you are, the more effective you will be in the long run.

Learning to design and code are two key parts of learning how to build. There are also several non-technical projects that can teach you how to build and become an effective startup product manager. In the next chapter, we will focus on the importance of building businesses and how it can help you become a startup product manager. Building a business can help you break into startup product management, become a better startup product manager, and learn business strategy through execution.

CHAPTER 10

WHY YOU SHOULD BUILD A BUSINESS AS A PRODUCT MANAGER

In this chapter, I want to focus on **why** building a business or side project is tremendously valuable for current and aspiring startup product managers. Pursuing entrepreneurial pursuits can accelerate your career significantly as a startup product manager. Building a business can help you land a job in startup product management, teach you how to be a startup product manager before you become one, equip you with valuable skill sets, and open doors for you throughout your career.

The Secret to Becoming An Effective Product Manager: Build a Business or Side Project

1. Why building a business (or side project) can help you become the most effective startup product manager you can be:

I would highly recommend starting a business or side project, regardless of your background. At their core, startup product managers are entrepreneurs. At an early-stage startup, you work within strict constraints: you have limited resources to solve a challenging problem and build a product that will help grow a business. As a result, startup product managers have to constantly adapt and find innovative ways to prioritize. They have to invest their time wisely and determine the most effective uses of it in order to scale a company. Ultimately, you are also under significant pressure: startups are fast-paced, and funding is limited. To prepare for startup product management, you should consider building your own business. Building a business from scratch may be even more difficult because you may have to bootstrap it, and in that way, it will prepare you even more for becoming a startup product manager. Further, if you are already a startup product manager, you should consider building a business. Building your own business is one of the best ways to hone your adaptability and product sense. Especially at an early stage startup, you **have** to adapt as a product manager. Product managers who have an entrepreneurial background, combined with an understanding of the fundamentals of product and business strategy, accelerate quickly in startup product management. An entrepreneurial background teaches you the mindset of "do anything to get the job done." You constantly have to be scrappy and be creative in your approach for solving problems. Further, entrepreneurs focus on the top priorities. Entrepreneurs take pride in doing what no one else wants to do. However, at the same time, they do the less glamorous work because they know it will move the needle forward for their companies. Entrepreneurs also know they cannot work on everything, so they develop an intuition for delegation and know how to empower their team members to achieve goals as well. When you have an entrepreneurial background along with building skills (design and coding), it will set you apart as a startup product manager.

Entrepreneurial experience is a gift that helps you build a unique mindset. It is the mindset that matters here, more than the skills. I have seen product managers with an entrepreneurial background have a greater self-awareness of their strengths. Entrepreneurial individuals gravitate towards their strengths, yet they are always willing to try new things. And trying new things may mean failing at them. But these entrepreneurial individuals never give up. They keep going until they find a solution or an answer to a problem. They keep tinkering, optimizing, and experimenting until they find what works. Startup product managers with an entrepreneurial background capitalize on their strengths, while having the optimism to learn new skills. In order to be successful as a startup product manager, you need to play to your strengths and have the openness to continue learning new abilities that will help you in the role.

When you are faced with challenges in multiple directions, you need to have the grit and tenacity to keep going — as well as the flexibility to learn new things. These are all core parts of being an entrepreneur.

How to Effectively Learn Product And Business Strategy

2. Why building a business can help you learn about product and business strategy:

Product and business strategy are skills that are **built** over time. Through experience, you gain an intuition and perspective into how to approach certain situations after consistent execution for multiple years. Product sense is built through identifying problems that customers have and solving them. Specifically, it involves building different products, testing products/apps/services, using competitor products, learning from other builders, and observing human behavior. Product sense is the ability to connect the dots to find answers and think creatively based on your knowledge and the knowledge you seek. When you are building a side project or a business, you are crafting the initial dots that you will end up connecting later on. **Strategy** comes from **experience**, which comes from **execution**. Adopting a growth mindset towards product and business strategy will help you succeed and be more open to learning as a startup product manager.

There are certain skills and concepts that you learn by **doing** that will make you a better startup product manager. Product managers at early stage startups have to wear multiple hats and be scrappy. If you have built side projects, you likely have been a product manager before — regardless of whether or not you officially had the title. Product management is about identifying problems, collaborating with people to find solutions, and acting on those solutions.

How to Become a Problem Solver: The Practicality of Building a Business

3. Here is why it is practical to build a business:

Today, as a startup product manager, I draw directly from my experiences building businesses and side projects in the past. Working on a business can be a great way to gain practical experience. When you start a business, you are typically building a product or service from the ground up. When you build a product or service, **you are solving a problem** for someone or something. A product has to provide value for the end user in order to be successful. Value is subjective and how you define it. As you build a product over time, you have to think through the go-to-market. Product and distribution go hand in hand. That product or service must follow through with execution on the go-to-market side, whether it involves content creation, partnerships, SEO, etc. After you perform an initial launch, you listen to feedback from your initial customers and then continue to iterate on it. Building a business gives you a founder mindset, and that is what differentiates good from great startup product managers. Startup product managers can often get in the weeds of execution. It requires effort to take a step back and evaluate the business from a strategic lens. Repeated execution will help inform how you may shape the strategic vision of a business, and you need to take time to exercise your muscle of analyzing your business from an aerial view. The ways you can exercise this muscle are by building a business yourself and by investigating the strategic vision of the startup you work at. When you begin to think about the future of the business, how the product relates to growth of the business, and the top priorities of a business, you adopt a higher-level view of the startup.

My side projects throughout the years have included YouTube channels, ecommerce businesses, digital products, blogs, and small startups. Some have been successful at different levels, some have been failures. In every situation, I learned something new and took that to the next opportunity. All you have to do is start. The secret to finding your next business idea is to look at your past experiences, your current interests, and the opportunities in the market.

You start by identifying a problem in the world, and you can create a high-impact opportunity for yourself by solving that problem. Once you solve it well, you can continue to solve other problems. And you continue to repeat that cycle over time. The best part is that there are no strict rules, beyond the rules that these platforms have. You need to create a great product **and** distribute it. You can create anything: whether that is a YouTube or TikTok channel, an eBay business, a business inside a multiplayer video game, an Etsy store, a tutoring business, etc. It can be anything! Here is the business idea matrix for discovering or building your own business.

The Business Idea Matrix

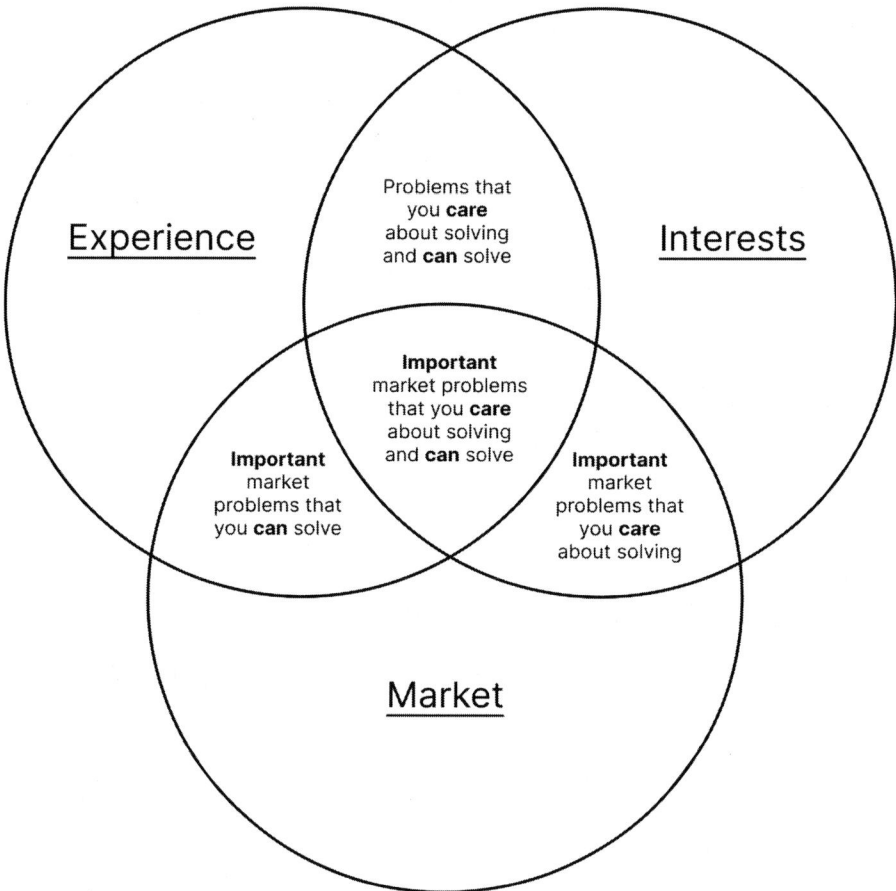

Experience

Interests

Problems that you **care** about solving and **can** solve

Important market problems that you **care** about solving and **can** solve

Important market problems that you **can** solve

Important market problems that you **care** about solving

Market

Here are a few resources that can help you brainstorm business ideas as well:

- *Ali Abdaal:* How to Start a Business from NOTHING
- *Ali Abdaal:* How I Built 9 Streams of Income By 23

Businesses do not need software to scale, but software can help scale businesses. Your business idea does not have to be technical and does not need to require design or development. You can also use no-code tools that exist on the market to help build your business. If you are comfortable with software, you can build a business with software. However, creating software is not the only way to solve a problem. Software can help facilitate scalable solutions, but you do not have to start out with a software business model. You should focus most of your time on understanding the problem you want to solve very deeply, and then once you do understand it, you can then start building solutions around it.

Business ideas can draw from one of your hobbies, your past experiences personally or professionally, or opportunities in the market. The importance should be on solving problems for your end user and continuing to make your product & distribution better. Getting started is the hardest part.

Here is great advice from Justin Kan, the founder of Twitch, on how to get started doing anything: *Justin Kan:* How To Get Started Doing Anything

How to Get Customers to Love Your Business and Product

4. Focus on your customers and get them to their "aha" moment:

When you are starting a business or side project, you should focus on your customers and get them to their **"aha" moment**. This is a widely spoken concept in product. You need to understand a customer's problem, solve that problem through your product well, help the customer see the value, and secure the customer as an adopter of your product. Every time a customer uses your product, you need to understand all sides of the story. If the customer liked your product, you need to understand what went well. If the customer is ecstatic about your product, you need to understand what they are passionate about. If your customer disliked your product, you need to understand what did not go well. You need to collect all of this feedback and continue to iterate on it. Every customer that uses your product does not need to love your product, but you have to find a few that do love your product. And for those who love your product, you need to continue solving problems for them. In order to get new customers, you need to continue identifying and solving new problems that are out in the market. Businesses are built on identifying problems in the market, solving problems for customers, and creating solutions that customers love. In order to become a great startup product manager, you should build your own business or side project and do all three of those things. The more repetitions you get in this process, the more you understand what it takes to get a customer to their "aha" moment.

You learn from each experience and use it to more effectively handle the next experience. Although no two experiences are the same, you begin to develop a perspective on what matters the most when it comes to building. These entrepreneurial experiences you gain through building businesses or side projects will continue to benefit you as a startup product manager throughout your career journey.

The Top Business Principles And Strategies You Need to Know as a Startup Product Manager

5. Why studying previous businesses and business models are crucial:

In order to become a good startup product manager, you need to learn how to execute and be tactical. However, in order to become the best startup product manager you can be, you need to be a strategic thinker and learn the fundamentals of business. There are many ways to become a strategic thinker and learn business fundamentals: it can be valuable for you to study how successful businesses, products, and services have been created. Why is this important? Startup product managers need to have structured thinking and communicate the startup's strategic initiatives with the rest of the organization. In order for your team members to effectively execute, you have to develop a clear vision for them. Developing a clear vision is built on how well you, as a startup product manager, understand the business and how well you can align teams on the overall strategy. Your leadership is perceived based on how well you deliver customer and business context to your team members, as well as how well you can align cross-functional teams to achieve their goals. When you communicate with your go-market, design, and engineering counterparts, you need to tell a story about what customer problems you are solving for and why they are important to the business. Your team members need to understand and become invested in the startup vision. In order for you to achieve that, it helps that you understand how businesses are built and learn the principles of business. Startup product managers also need to influence without authority. They need to manage up with the executive team and manage across different teams. The way you influence without authority is by having a deep understanding of the business. When you fundamentally understand where the business is heading, you can prioritize your own initiatives and align teams better. In order to manage up, you need to understand what is fundamentally important to executive stakeholders in the company. Typically, they invest their time into defining how they will grow revenue, acquire new customers, and shape the business strategy. When you understand what they care about, you can then influence more effectively without authority and move the business in the right direction. Startup product managers who understand business principles and strategy can more effectively communicate with executive stakeholders, understand the vision, influence the vision, and create alignment across cross-functional teams to achieve that vision.

The Startup Product Manager's Ten Business Principles	
Customers	How well do you understand your customers' problems, any issues with how they may be solved currently, and how you can solve them more effectively?
Competitors	How well do you understand your competitors' strengths and weaknesses, the products and services they offer, and how they differentiate themselves?
Market	How well do you understand the size of the market your startup is in, the growth of the market you are in, your competitive advantages in the market, and if your startup plans to expand into other markets?
Product	How well do you understand your startup's core value proposition, how your product is unique, and what the product roadmap involves?
Pricing	How well do you understand how your product will be priced, how your startup structures its current business model (B2B, B2C, B2B2C), how the original business model will evolve over time, how much your customers will pay for your product, and how switching costs

	will affect your customers' decisions when choosing a product?
Differentiation	How well do you understand how your startup will diversify its revenue streams, how it will stand out in the market, how it will plan to increase the customer lifetime value, and how it will identify/prioritize new opportunities?
Stakeholders	How well do you understand the key internal and external players for your startup, how these individuals or entities influence the business, and what impact would these stakeholders have in product development?
Mission	How well do you understand why your startup is doing what it is doing, the values of the startup, and the long-term vision of the startup?
Targets	How well do you understand the key objectives and metrics of your startup, the goals your startup wants to hit both in the near-term and long-term, and how you can align your product strategy with the targets that are set?
Invested Capital	How well do you understand where and how your startup is investing its resources (hiring new employees, growing/retaining current employees, customer acquisition, customer activation, customer retention, strategic partnerships), how much your startup is spending, and the reasons behind these investment decisions?

As a startup product manager, you need to supplement what you learn on the job with what you learn from studying businesses that have succeeded (or failed) previously. Most who became great at anything had to go beyond what they could learn on their own. They took their time to study the greats in their field, worked with others who made up for their weaknesses, were advised by other startup operators, or had mentorship from those with experience.

Here is a framework for learning business strategy from others:

1. Understand what you are specifically trying to learn more about and how it impacts business strategy. Find the niche term(s) for the concept you are trying to learn about.

2. Look up companies that succeeded using the specific strategies or concepts you are curious about.

3. Find the individuals who led high-impact initiatives at these companies, affected business strategy, and helped the companies scale.

4. Discover content that these individuals have created: written, visual, audio (blog posts, newsletters, YouTube videos, podcasts, interviews, etc).

5. Take learnings from these individuals and use that to dive deeper into concepts you are curious about by finding more content online that were created by other individuals.

6. Using what you have learned from others, you can test and apply what you can on the job as a startup product

manager to see if it fits within the context of your company. If it works, it works. If it does not work, it does not work. You have to consistently validate your hypotheses and find what does work.

7. Measure outcomes, keep testing, and continue to build your knowledge over time to create the best product you can.

For instance, you may be interested in "growth" as a product manager and want to learn more about it. You could look up companies that have scaled by creating systems of growth over time. Meta (Facebook) is one example of a company that constructed a growth team and scaled to billions of users. You can find the individuals that led growth at Facebook in its early days and discover content online that they have created. When you get a higher level understanding of the concepts they talk about in the content you find online, you can continue to build upon your learnings from them. You can discover new content related to the concepts they discuss. When you feel comfortable with a concept discussed, you can apply it on the job. You can test it, validate it, and measure the results. You can keep trying to figure out what works best for your startup. Now, it is not that cut and dry. There are nuances to how you apply business strategy from other contexts into the context of your startup. This is the general approach you can take for applying what you learn off the job to what you do on the job.

As a startup product manager, you need to develop your product intuition over time in two ways: through gaining practical experience and applying learnings from others. This will give you context into how to create a successful product and business. You do not need to identically follow any particular frameworks or copy what other people have done. Every business is built differently. You should use other strategies as inspiration rather than necessarily copying them.

These are additional frameworks, principles, and strategies that will help you as a startup product manager:

- Amazon's Leadership Principles: (Google "Amazon's Principles")
- Porter's 5 Forces: (Google "Porter's 5 Forces Diagram")
- The SaaS Metrics That Matter by David Sacks and Ethan Ruby
- The Business Model Canvas

I want to preface by saying the following: **your ability to develop strategy comes through experience and learning**. As a startup product manager, you will naturally become more strategic by learning how to execute well first and then relate your execution back to the goals of business. Learning from others can supplement your learning on the job. You learn the most through real-world execution.

CHAPTER 11

THE POWER OF VERBAL COMMUNICATION FOR STARTUP PRODUCT MANAGERS

Verbal communication is one of the greatest skills that anyone can develop over time. At early-stage startups, given the flat organizational structure, your ability to communicate will help set you apart. Startup product managers communicate with nearly everyone in the company. This alone makes it that much more important to know why you should be developing your communication skills. In this chapter, I will focus on reasons **why** verbal communication is valuable for startup product managers. Verbal communication as a product manager involves both written and spoken communication. Some may gravitate towards one or another, but both are equally important. This chapter will focus on spoken communication, and the next chapter will focus on written communication. These are life-long skills that anyone can improve on.

Six Habits of Great Spoken Communicators

1. Any product manager can be great at spoken communication. Great communicators constantly work on their craft.

Spoken communication is a learnable skill that can be crafted and honed over time. There is no one archetype of a successful startup product manager. Those who consider themselves introverts or extroverts have succeeded in this role, and both have been exceptional. The most exceptional communicators may seem as if spoken communication comes naturally to them. Often, it is quite the opposite. They spend years and years getting better at communication, through doing self-assessments of their communication skills and also learning from others who they feel communicate well. The main characteristic that makes exceptional communicators great is their curiosity for learning how to provide value for others when they do communicate and their constant initiative for growing their own skills. From my past experiences and from talking to many product managers, there are a few key traits I have observed that make product managers great spoken communicators. I want to provide you with a framework for becoming a great spoken communicator. This is what I believe is valuable:

- First, they listen. This is the most important part. In order to deliver an important message, you must listen to the person or the people you are talking to. Great startup product managers understand people and gain context. You need to understand what is important to those who you are communicating with. Startup product managers are the glue that holds an organization together and the engine that drives an organization forward. When you understand what is fundamentally important to your stakeholders, you will learn more about who they are and how you can potentially help them. You should aim to provide value to them and learn to give without expecting anything in return. Use spoken communication as a tool for generosity: providing context, communicating goals, aligning on expectations, unblocking teams, giving updates, and empowering people to do great work.

- When great communicators speak, they speak clearly. They speak at their natural pace and with limited filler words. It is important to think through what you say and then say it clearly. It helps to slow down when talking and think through what you plan to say. Identify the ideal natural pace for yourself. You need to have control over your pace of speaking: there are certain situations where you want to speed up your pace and other situations where you want to slow down your pace. When you explain something, you are going to want to slow down when you talk. However, when you are trying to inspire your team, you may want to get your initial message across slowly and then talk faster to generate enthusiasm around your idea. You need to be able to speak clearly and think about what you say before you say it.

- Confidence is key. You must believe in what you are saying. If you have a certain point of view, you can back it up with evidence and facts. You should not doubt yourself if you are making the time and effort to say something. If you do not know something, then confidently say you do not know it. For instance, you may have a question from a stakeholder in a meeting. It is hard to have an answer to everything. You can always ask follow-up questions and get back to someone with an answer after that meeting. It is okay to not know everything. Startup product managers play the role of visionary and guide execution, so you need to own the end to end process. You need to find answers to unanswered questions and unblock your teams as time permits. You need to **believe** in what you are building, why you are building it, and the story you are telling to your team. As mentioned earlier, context is key. Your ability to communicate context confidently will make you a great startup product manager.
- Small talk is a great way to connect with your team. You can talk about hobbies, ask someone about their day at the beginning of a conversation, and learn more about what excites and drives your team members. You need to create an environment that facilitates the best ideas and creativity. It helps build a better culture for your team when

you develop a genuine interest in what your team members are interested in. The more you can find common ground, the more fun work will be for you and those who you work with.

- You do not need to speak all the time. Great product managers empower others and contribute to conversations when needed. You do not need to dominate a conversation. You do need to flow with the conversation. The opinions of others are just as important as yours. Learning to step back and know when to talk is a skill that comes with time, but this is critical to being a good teammate and good startup product manager.

- Simplify your content. Avoid complex words and jargon. Talk in a way that anyone can understand what you are saying. It is important to explain and provide context, but remembering to be concise and easily understood is just as important. The smartest and most successful startup product managers use simple language. They break down complex problems and solutions in terms that anyone can understand. You are the translator across the whole organization. Your words carry value, and you do not need complex words to communicate complex concepts. You need to use simple words to communicate complex concepts. Your use of simple language helps you solve problems with teams efficiently, create alignment across different teams quickly, and execute with teams effectively.

Why Spoken Communication is Important for Startup Product Managers

2. Meetings are an important part of a product manager's job. Spoken communication is the core foundation of helping meetings run well.

As a product manager, your schedule will involve a lot of meetings. In these meetings, you need to listen and talk to various teams. Often, these meetings exist with your internal and external stakeholders. Internally, you will have different types of meetings: you will have standups with your engineers and designers to talk through updates, brainstorming sessions across different teams to create solutions to problems, syncs with your go-to-market teams to understand analytics or customer feedback (marketing, customer success, and sales teams), discussions with other product managers to share product changes or align on processes, 1 on 1s with your manager to talk through what is top of mind for you, and presentations to provide updates to executive stakeholders. Externally, you will have meetings as well: you will talk to customers (it can include user research, discovery, user testing, etc), create partnerships with other brands for your product, talk to vendors to discover new software collaborations, or work with other businesses involved in your product strategy. Your effectiveness in spoken communication will drive your ability to prioritize important topics in meetings and effectively manage your time. There are tactical ways to become a better spoken communicator, and we will cover these steps in the next section.

How to Become a Clear Communicator

3. These are the exact steps you can take to become a clear communicator as a product manager.

Product managers should learn how to speak publicly in front of groups and speak with clarity, confidence, concision, and empathy. I recommend improving as a speaker in two ways initially: study how **you** speak and study how **others** speak.

You need to do a self-assessment on how you communicate:

1. How well do you listen to others in meetings?
2. Do you speak clearly in meetings?
3. Do you have awareness of your natural pace when speaking?
4. Are you able to communicate with your team in a concise manner?
5. How confident are you when you talk in meetings?
6. How often do you stop to let others speak?
7. How often do you speak during meetings?
8. Do you make an effort to learn more about your team members, such as their professional interests at work and personal hobbies outside of work? Being a good communicator involves being a good human first.

9. Are you intentional with your communication and try to add value?

10. Do you make an effort to learn what is important to your team members and try to find ways to help them?

11. Do you use simple language that is easy to understand when talking to team members?

If you record your meetings and re-watch how you talk in meetings, you can pick up on nuances of how you currently communicate. There is always more to learn, and you can always become a better communicator. You can ask a teammate for feedback and ask the following questions: *How did this meeting go? How was the message delivered? What do you think we could have improved on?*

Further, you can observe how influential leaders communicate well. You need to have professionalism when communicating, but you also should be yourself. It is important to be professional: clear, concise, thoughtful, confident, and empathetic. Beyond performing a self-assessment on your communication style, you can also study interviews of successful leaders who communicate well:

- I particularly recommend Stanford GSB's speaker series on YouTube, *View From The Top*: https://bit.ly/3CpGANt

There are several other ways to improve how you communicate. Your verbal intuition is built from living day to day. You do not become a better communicator solely through work. Outside of work, in your current role, you can join a team or do group activities. Learning how to be a great communicator involves learning how to be a great team player first. You can engage in team sports, play video games, volunteer in your local community, or take a fun class. There are so many lessons you will learn about being a great leader and communicator from other environments. If you are in college, you can take a leadership role in an extracurricular club and work in a team. You will learn about spoken communication through organizations you participate in, classes you take, and people you meet. Whether you are a full-time professional, a student, or anyone else, you can find creative ways to improve your spoken communication.

Spoken communication is one of the most valuable skills to improve on as a startup product manager. As mentioned earlier, your spoken and written communication skills go hand in hand to help you become the best startup product manager you can be. Wherever you go in your career, verbal communication will take you far as a core skill set. There is endless learning and opportunity to grow. With everything, it takes practice.

CHAPTER 12

WHY WRITING IS YOUR ULTIMATE STRENGTH AS A STARTUP PRODUCT MANAGER

Writing can be your greatest asset as a startup product manager. All product managers should master writing clearly and concisely. Writing helps you become a more effective leader and thinker. It helps you process ideas and communicate plans into words that everyone can understand. In today's hybrid (primarily virtual) work environment, it is even more important to write.

As a startup product manager, you will be working with multiple teams on a daily basis. Establishing a writing culture in your organization is important. Writing facilitates cross-functional work, knowledge transfer, and context-building. A top concern many product managers have is that they are always in meetings. If you can master the art of written communication, you can provide value without meetings and grow your ability to say "no" to meetings over time. Great writing is not a cure-all for every problem or meeting, but it has helped many product managers work more effectively and efficiently. Some situations require meetings, so having the ability to speak and write well are equally important. Writing can help you save time when done well. You can convey and communicate through concise updates, while getting stakeholder input and helping everyone feel involved.

Startup product management is a game of time and focus. The better you can manage your time, the better you can focus your energy towards identifying and executing on the most important problems. Writing will help you have more control of your time: it is a skill that will help you stand out, deliver impactful results, and provide more balance in your day-to-day life as a product manager. Startup product management involves driving outcomes for your business and for your customers. The more you grow skills that help you manage your time, the more energy you can dedicate towards your top priorities as a startup product manager. Writing is one of those skills that will help you manage your time. The more you can execute on the top priorities for the company, the greater the impact you will have. We will dive more into why writing is important and how to improve your writing in this chapter.

The Keys to Masterfully Navigating Time Management and Modern Stakeholder Management

1. Written communication is the cornerstone of effective stakeholder management.

Learning how to communicate **well** through writing will set you apart from the pack as a startup product manager. Today, the startup industry continues to operate in a hybrid or remote-first environment where a greater portion of your communication will not be in person. In your current role, you may use communication software on a frequent basis with your team members right now. At a startup, when your team members are in different time zones or different areas of the world, you will often have to write as a way to communicate. Meetings can be a supplemental way to create the foundation or help further deliver an understanding of what you already write down. Written communication increasingly will be the skill that differentiates you as a startup product manager.

Stakeholder management is one of the many keys to being a successful product manager. Arguably, it can be the most important skill (especially in startups) as your company continues to scale and grow over time. In order to become great at stakeholder management, you need to master verbal communication. Given that startup environments are becoming more asynchronous, you need to invest more into developing your written communication skills.

On a daily basis, you are communicating with several stakeholders internally and externally. Internal stakeholders exist across different departments in the organization. This includes your direct team as well as adjacent teams that you interact with. As a startup product manager, you are the bridge that holds different units together. Internally, you will work across your go-to-market teams, design teams, engineering teams, and beyond. When you write once, you can share it everywhere. Sometimes meetings can be easier: you may be leading brainstorming sessions, giving presentations to executives, talking about metrics and goals, or providing a product demo to team members. As a startup product manager, you will always have an opportunity to speak with your internal stakeholders. It is your job to prioritize which opportunities make sense to have meetings for and which do not make sense. Writing can help save you time. Startup product managers can use their written communication skills to build understanding and share context across different teams, as well as collaborate with them offline.

Externally, startup product managers also have significant influence when it comes to interacting with stakeholders outside of their companies. Your customers and strategic partners will be the two external groups that startup product managers interact with the most. Startup product managers prioritize problems to solve for and address the needs of customers. Startup product managers also need to work with strategic partners to help expand the reach of their startups by helping you gain entry into new networks and establishing a joint competitive advantage. For customers and strategic partners, depending on the context, there is no set rule to whether you should use spoken or written communication. What matters is having a great relationship with your customers or your business partners because they will also help drive your startup forward. Generally, you should adapt to the communication style that they prefer. Listening to their preferred communication style will help grow your relationship further. You need to have a mix of great spoken and written communication skills. You will often interact directly with customers through your communication software or by email, so you should be at the top of your game when it comes to writing. They have limited time, and you need to find a solution to their problems and questions as soon as possible. Crafting a quality response in a short time period is the key to providing value to customers. Especially at B2B startups, when you get to develop closer relationships over time with specific customers, you need to master this skill. On the other hand, you may have strategic relationships with external business partners. You also need to be prompt in your communication, but your written communication needs to be top notch in order to create trust through being a professional and by providing value to them.

The best startup product managers are those who understand how to effectively and efficiently communicate with stakeholders, both internally and externally. The ability to write well will provide you with more autonomy over your time. Learning how to manage your time well as a startup product manager will serve as a strategic advantage for the rest of your career. Written communication plays a key role in time management and stakeholder management. In order to level up as a product manager, you need to know when to communicate through writing and when to supplement it with speaking.

Why Writing is a Daily Necessity for Product Managers

2. Writing is a core part of most of your day-to-day responsibilities.

The responsibilities of a startup product manager can include talking to customers, discovering new problem spaces, brainstorming opportunities, prioritizing new initiatives, building out the product roadmap, running sprints, writing user stories, unblocking team members, writing about feature releases, messaging all kinds of internal & external stakeholders, outlining product requirements in a document, monitoring metrics, studying competitors, conducting market research, and coordinating product launches. All of these responsibilities involve writing.

Product management goes beyond "building." There is so much more that goes beyond shipping features. Startup product managers have to master the craft of distribution as well. You can build a product, but you need to find a way to get customers to come. For most products, you have to find where your customers are and tell them about your product. Startup product managers need to talk to internal and external stakeholders about product launches, do feature demos, measure the success of product launches, work alongside go-to-market teams to create a vision for selling the product and onboarding users. While you need to build products in a compelling way that actually solves the needs of customers, you also need to craft a narrative around these products that generates excitement. You need to imagine your products being talked about on tech blogs, social media, review platforms, and more. Startup product managers are the orchestrators that build products and sell the vision. They sell the vision through verbal communication. Your ability to write in a compelling way can frame how customers and other stakeholders view the products you launch. Startup product managers need to become experts in interpersonal communication. It is just as important to learn the adjacent soft skills. Emotional intelligence is key as a startup product manager. You need to anticipate your stakeholders' behaviors, be aware of their needs, and be ready to deliver updates to them. With more experience, you will be able to anticipate situations and be able to quickly adapt. Working with various teams involves cross-functional alignment and building the intuition to know what is important to them.

Over time, your goal is to learn how to effectively influence stakeholders without being the direct leader of those teams. Influencing without authority can come through strong written communication, and you will be able to help others see that you are a team player that drives the vision forward. Mastering written communication will not only help the company succeed but also benefit your career trajectory.

Product Diplomacy: Why Written Communication is The Secret to Building a Strong Product, Business, And Culture

2. Startups need product managers to be diplomats and strong communicators who align teams to drive the product vision forward.

As a product manager, you are the diplomat of your organization. You need to bring parties together and solve problems together. You need to decide what problems are important to solve, why you should solve those problems, and provide context for those problems to your team. As a company grows over time, context is often delivered through written communication. In order to build trust with your team, they need to have context: they want to know why certain problems are being solved, why features are being built in the ways they are, how they play a role in delivering an impact for the company and its customers, why any strategic decisions are made, and how they can be a part of the future vision. Writing helps you build an aligned culture, which becomes an unstoppable force that can solve any problem, build any product, and drive the business forward. Delivering context is how you create teams that feel invested and confident in the mission. When your teams have context, which you can deliver by writing either through documentation or communication, you are able to align your teams. When teams are aligned, you can build a better product, business, and culture.

As an example, the next time you work with your design and engineering counterparts, you should take a step back and think about the context you can provide. Instead of saying "deliver feature X in this sprint," you can talk about **why** that feature is important to deliver, **what** problem it is solving, and **who** it is important for. Startup product managers focus on the problems that customers are facing and why those problems are important to solve. It is critical that your designers and engineers understand this as well, so that they build the best product with the right context and intent in mind.

Before you build features as a startup product manager, you need to thoughtfully think through the problem prior to executing on any ideas and solutions. You need to be an expert on the problem. Startup product managers identify the problem space for a given set of customers, prioritize the problems they want to solve for these customers, inspire their teams to get excited about the important problems, brainstorm solutions with their teams, and empower their teams to execute on those solutions. You need to tell the overall story of why a problem is important to solve. Your team will then figure out **how** to solve a problem. It is your job to communicate why it is important to solve a problem and to collaborate with them to best solve that problem as a team.

As a startup product manager, you have to constantly problem-solve and grow your brainstorming abilities to build products. These skills are just as important as your ability to inform, communicate, and bring people together. Startup product management is like directing a movie. You have to write the script, direct the film, set the foundation for the story, and trust your stars to shine. Distribution is important: you need to market your film before the launch and after the launch, create a compelling preview to the film, and partner with distribution channels to execute on your paid and organic strategies as well as ensure that people hear about your film. Writing is the key to building products and mastering distribution. Writing helps you keep these moving pieces together and produce a great product for your audience.

Writing is one of the fundamental keys to startup success for product managers. As a startup product manager, you have to understand how to build a product and how to sell a product vision. If you understand how to build and how to communicate well, it will not only take you far in your career as a product manager but also open up opportunities for you in other aspects of your life. Writing gives you leverage. Mastering writing is the key to fast-tracking your career and becoming a successful product manager.

Now, how do you become a better writer? There are tactical strategies we will cover soon, and they will help you become a better written communicator as a startup product manager and for the rest of your career.

Seven Steps on How to Improve Your Writing as a Product Manager

3. How you can become a better writer.

1. **Start writing**. In order to become better at writing, you just have to get started. And then you have to keep going. Everyone starts somewhere. If your goal is to become a better writer, you should write in public. You can write in public by writing on the internet or at work. This way, you can get feedback from potential readers and continue to iterate on your writing style. As a startup product manager, your writing will be highly visible with various stakeholders in your company. You will play a role in setting the standard for written communication at your company. It is important to get comfortable with writing in public because it is a core part of your day to day work as a startup product manager.

2. **Develop your voice**. In order to become confident in your writing, you have to be yourself. You have to write without worrying about what other people think. The truth is, early on, most writers will not have many individuals reading their initial writing. An audience that trusts you and

consistently returns to your content is gradually developed over time. It will take time before you develop a following or have many people read what you write. Also, you can always delete your writing or make it private if you want to hide it online. You should be comfortable being yourself when you write. Once you get to a point when readers start to publicly give feedback on your writing or share your writing online, you will start to understand that your writing has had an impact on others. Ultimately, your writing has to mean something to yourself first in order to get there. Once you find your own voice, you can then give meaning to your writing. As long as *you* care about your writing, you will eventually find others who deeply care about your writing as well. Everyone will write differently, so do what best suits you. Learning to write with clarity and purpose is what has helped the most as a product manager.

3. **Study how others write**. You can read almost anything and take inspiration from everything. Reading creative pieces will help you learn how to become a better storyteller. Reading blogs or newsletters will help you learn how to deliver points concisely. Reading about sports allows you to understand how to incorporate insights from an event or discuss highlights. It can be anything. Learning how to craft a narrative, position a topic, and provide context are all parts of product management. Writing is a

life-long skill in which you can learn from others and use it as a way to continue developing your writing style.

4. **Pick one thing to get better every time you write. Use this principle to find content-market fit.** Every time you write, you should read your most recent writing and think about one thing you can improve on the next time you write. You have to go back to your old writing: reflect on what you did well, as well as what you did not do well. It also helps to send your writing to others and get feedback. Typically, when you write in public, you will know if you wrote well. When we talk about writing "well," it is in the context of creating valuable content that your audience cares about. Once you define your audience, you are then able to double down and continue delivering content to expand your reach as well as deliver new value-added content. In the beginning, you may have to brute force your way to finding an audience by actively sharing your writing products on social media. When you find even a select few readers who enjoy your content, you will know that you have found content-market fit. Writing well involves communicating the message in a way that makes others feel invested in its purpose. Your writing needs to evoke something in the reader. When readers react and are responsive to your writing, you will know that your writing is clear and makes sense. If people are quiet around your writing, you may not have clarity in your writing or provide

enough value through your writing. Alternatively, it may be a sign that you have not distributed your content effectively enough. It helps to continuously check in with yourself: you need to understand how you feel as a writer and creator, and you need to evaluate whether your audience is receptive to your content. You need to perform a self-assessment of your writing and pick one small thing to get better at. For example, if you are writing a blog post, you can focus on creating a better headline. The next time, you can focus on how you organize different sections of your blog post. After this, you can focus on the introduction of your blog post and how you will grab the attention of your readers. Later, you can think about how to create calls to action and tell your audience to do something. Further, you can read comments from your readers and learn how to anticipate new topics that they may want to read about. There are always steps you can take to improve your writing.

5. **Narrow down on a niche and then expand from there.** I started writing for fun about startups, venture capital, and product management. You could write about anything. You may have an interest in writing about your favorite hobbies (TV shows, movies, sports, music), documenting your career or personal life, telling creative stories that you personally create, reviewing products and services, teaching people about a skill, and many more things. And

you build up your writing skills over time. The best time to start writing is now. It is never too late to begin. Similar to building a product, you can target one market when you write: you can write about a niche within a particular space or industry. As you feel more comfortable, you can continue to explore other markets and expand your writing to cover multiple niches. Once you write about one niche, you can always write about other niches. The reason I recommend focusing on one niche to start is because you can quickly test whether you enjoy writing about it, understand how well your content is received, and identify any future opportunities for writing more content. If one niche performs particularly well for you to start, you can start there and then pivot later. I highly encourage you to test other niches but to remain focused in the beginning.

6. **Be consistent.** You need to write multiple times and keep writing for consistency. This is where most people give up. If you can consistently write, you will become more comfortable with your own style. The way to keep learning is to keep writing. You can write once a week, once a month, or another interval depending on your comfort level and the type of content you write.

7. **Experiment.** You should keep trying new things in your writing. Your "style" is not a constant style, and it can constantly evolve over time. The core voice of who you are may stay similar over time, but you may want to

experiment with how you write and what you write about. You may consider taking creative risks. In order to experiment, you can create a roadmap, a vision board, or a backlog of ideas that you want to experiment with in the future. The ways you can get ideas for experimenting with your writing can involve reading comments from your readers, reading comments from other similar published content that you find, talking to your readers, finding similar content (podcasts, blogs, books, etc), studying your competitors if there are any within your space, and taking inspiration from anything you find interesting. There are many ways you can experiment with your writing. You should be creative day to day, but you should be strategic month to month. Have a plan for execution when it comes to your writing, and do not be afraid to leave your comfort zone. Trying new things is where you learn the most in writing and grow.

You can view writing as a product that you can distribute. Writing is a skill and an asset that will help you in your career as a startup product manager. Learning how to become the best writer you can be will help you hone in on your ultimate strength as a product manager.

CHAPTER 13

THE TOP PRODUCT MANAGERS WHO YOU CAN FOLLOW FOR FREE AND WILL HELP YOU BECOME GREAT

One of the most effective ways to scale up in your career as a startup product manager is to follow and learn from experienced product managers. These are individuals who have once been in your shoes and can significantly help accelerate your career growth.

"When people tell me they've learned from experience, I tell them the trick is to learn from other people's experience." — Warren Buffet

https://quotefancy.com/quote/931086/Warren-Buffett-When-people-tell-me-they-ve-learned-from-experience-I-tell-them-the-trick

This chapter will reveal the top product managers who you can follow and learn from — **for free**. These are some of the top product managers who have provided enormous value to me in my career, and they can provide substantial value to you as well. They are product managers who have written content and created resources for anyone who has a desire to grow and become the best product manager they can be. Most of this information is free. The resources that these top product managers have created are timeless. What may take you months to learn can instead take you minutes. If you make an effort to read what they write or listen to what they talk about, you can learn much more quickly. All of these learnings compound over time. These are lessons and experiences that will continue to provide value regardless of the time and era you operate in as a startup product manager.

Granted, it is important to take what resonates with you and apply it to your day to day life. Not everything a product manager says online will be the truth for your situation. Truth is found in the nuances, and there are no shortcuts to learning. Your learnings from their learnings will be highly context-specific. These product managers have worked in similar or different environments to yours. Their advice can vary based on the following factors: the industry of the startup, the venture stage of the startup, the business model of the startup, the level of product-market fit, the company size, the type of product management role, the types of products, the types of customers, the geography, the regulatory challenges, and more. There will be a lot of highly context-specific advice, so the lessons from a product manager who built one well-known startup may not all apply to the work you are doing. When you learn from many product managers, you need to employ connective thinking. The more product managers you follow, the more you will identify common themes from these product managers and leverage them. You will begin to identify patterns and fill in the knowledge gaps over time.

Learning from others' experiences is one of the best ways to learn. These practitioners and operators understand your journey; they have been in your shoes. They have failed, and they have succeeded. The ways to learn are through your experiences and through others' experiences. In order to grow the most, you need to acknowledge that there is always more to learn.

"Learn continually. There's always
"one more thing" to learn" — Steve Jobs.
https://quotefancy.com/quote/911572/Steve-Jobs-Learn-continually-There-s-always-one-more-thing-to-learn

The Top Product Managers You Can Learn From — Right Now

Lenny Rachitsky

1. Lenny Rachitsky: Founder of Lenny's Newsletter

Lenny Rachitsky is the founder of Lenny's Newsletter. He formerly founded a startup that was acquired by Airbnb and then led product teams, as well as growth initiatives at the company prior to its IPO. He currently writes on Twitter, publishes a newsletter, runs a community, hosts a podcast, teaches courses, and invests in startups in his free time. He helps several early and mid-career product managers and operators. Lenny's content and efforts have been some of the most influential in the entire product management ecosystem.

- Lenny's Twitter, Podcast, and Talent Collective:

  - https://twitter.com/lennysan
  - https://www.lennyspodcast.com/
  - https://www.lennysjobs.com/talent/welcome

- Lenny's Newsletter is "a weekly advice column about building product, driving growth, and working with humans."

  - https://www.lennysnewsletter.com/subscribe

- Lenny's "Product Management Fundamentals" Course *(ask if you can expense this at work)*:

  - https://maven.com/lenny/product-management-fundamentals

Shreyas Doshi

2. Shreyas Doshi: Advisor to fast-growing startups. ex-Stripe, Twitter, Google, Yahoo

Shreyas Doshi helped build products at Stripe, Twitter, Google, and Yahoo. He now writes across Linkedin and Twitter, advises startups in his free time, and teaches courses to help product managers grow. He creates several playbooks that product managers can follow, and he often gives them out for free on social media to his followers.

- Shreyas' Twitter and LinkedIn:
    - https://twitter.com/shreyas
    - https://www.linkedin.com/in/shreyasdoshi/

- Product Management learnings from Stripe, Yahoo, Google & Twitter | Shreyas Doshi | TPF:
    - Product Management learnings from Stripe, Yahoo, Google & Twitter | Shreyas Doshi | TPF

- Product Sense Workshop | ft. Kunal Shah and Shreyas Doshi | CRED
    - Product Sense Workshop | ft. Kunal Shah and Shreyas Doshi | CRED

Chloe Shih

2. Chloe Shih: Discord Product Manager | previously Meta, Google, TikTok, Caffeine | Content Creator

Chloe Shih is one of the leading content creators on YouTube for product management. She documents her career journey and learnings, with the goal of helping product managers and those who are interested in the space. Chloe has worked at Discord, Meta, Google, TikTok and Caffeine. She also has held many non-product management roles and understands the journey of breaking into product management from other backgrounds.

- Chloe's Twitter, YouTube, and Linkedin:

    - https://twitter.com/colorsofchloe
    - https://www.youtube.com/c/ColorsofChloe
    - https://www.linkedin.com/in/chloe-shih/

Jen Yang-Wong

3. Jen Yang-Wong: VP of Product @ Contrary | Angel Investor | ex-Uber

Jen Yang-Wong provides insightful advice on startups and product management on Twitter. She has worked at Contrary, Uber, and Novi in various product management roles. Jen provides strategic and tactical advice for product managers in their journey, whether it is in relation to their day to day work or overall career plan.

- Jen's Twitter and LinkedIn:

    - https://twitter.com/Jenyangwong
    - https://www.linkedin.com/in/jenniferyw/

Toby Rogers

4. Toby Rogers: Head of Product at hedgehog lab

Toby Rogers is currently the Head of Product at hedgehog lab and also one of the leading product management creators on Twitter. He writes straightforward advice and provides actionable lessons through his Twitter threads, as well as his newsletter.

- Toby's Twitter, Website, and LinkedIn:
    - https://twitter.com/tobiasrogers
    - https://tobyrogers.pm/
    - https://www.linkedin.com/in/tobiasrogers/

Jae Taylor

5. Jae Taylor: Founder @ MentorMesh

Jae Taylor is one of the top creators when it comes to professional development and identifying the top opportunities to progress your career. Jae previously worked in product and related roles at Peloton, Twitter, Salesforce, Microsoft, and Expedia. He founded MentorMesh to help those who are interested in advancing their careers in the tech industry. Jae provides free advice on Twitter and Linkedin to help individuals in their careers as well.

- Jae's Twitter and LinkedIn:
    - https://twitter.com/JaeOnTech

- https://www.linkedin.com/in/jaeintech/

Linda Zhang

6. Linda Zhang: Founder of Product Lessons

Linda Zhang is a solopreneur and former group product manager at Faire, a decacorn startup. She built the Product Toolkit and Product Lessons newsletter. Linda provides practical advice and discusses unique topics that are relevant to product managers, as well as many startup operators. She focuses on providing actionable advice that can tactically shape how you approach the next steps in your career.

- Linda's Twitter, *Product Lessons* newsletter (free), and Product Toolkit:

  - https://twitter.com/thelindazhang
  - https://www.productlessons.xyz/about
  - https://www.product-toolkit.com/

Jackie Bavaro

7. Jackie Bavaro: Author of Cracking the PM Interview and Cracking the PM Career, Previously Head of Product Management @ Asana, PM @ Google & Microsoft. She/Her

Jackie Bavaro is known for writing Cracking the PM Interview and Cracking the PM Career. She also previously led product management at Asana and worked at Google and Microsoft. Jackie has a wealth of experience that involves scaling startups, both in the form of revenue and product team sizes. She is a must-follow for any product manager.

- Jackie's Twitter and Medium:
  - https://twitter.com/jackiebo
  - https://jackiebo.medium.com/

- *Cracking the PM Career:* https://www.crackingthepmcareer.com/

- Exponent: Ace your Product Management Career with Jackie Bavaro, "Cracking The PM Interview" Author
  - Ace your Product Management Career with Jackie Bavaro, "Cracking The PM Interview" Author

Teresa Torres

8. Teresa Torres: Author, Speaker, Product Discovery Coach

Teresa Torres is a product coach and author who focuses on product discovery. She also advises individuals and startups through group and one-on-one efforts. Teresa also writes and gives advice for free on various social media platforms.

- Teresa's Twitter, Website, and LinkedIn
  - https://twitter.com/ttorres

- o https://www.producttalk.org/
- o https://www.linkedin.com/in/teresatorres/

Marty Cagan

9. Marty Cagan: Partner at Silicon Valley Product Group

Marty Cagan leads Silicon Valley Product Group and has written some of the most well-known books on product management. He focuses on mentoring product managers and companies to help them build better products. He is often featured on various platforms and attends events, providing advice to professionals on a frequent basis.

- Marty's Twitter, Website, and LinkedIn:

  - o https://twitter.com/cagan
  - o https://www.svpg.com/
  - o https://www.linkedin.com/in/cagan/

- Books: Inspired, Empowered

Aakash Gupta

10. Aakash Gupta: Former Group Product Manager at Affirm | Product Growth

Aakash Gupta writes about product growth and offers free advice, as well as case studies, through his various social media channels.

He has held product management roles at Affirm, Epic Games, Google, and many more companies. He is an entrepreneur and runs his own newsletter as well. If you are interested in growth and startups, he is a great person to learn from.

- Aakash's Twitter, LinkedIn, and Website:

    o https://twitter.com/aakashg0
    o https://www.linkedin.com/in/aagupta/
    o https://www.aakashg.com/

Ken Norton

11. Ken Norton: Executive Coach to Product Leaders

Ken currently serves as an executive coach to product and technology leaders. He provides timeless advice to product managers, and most of his content can be found on his website. You can also find publicly available content on YouTube from his various speaking engagements and interviews. Ken is one of the leading veterans in product management. He spent 14 years at Google as a product leader, leading initiatives for many important products.

- Ken's Website, Newsletter, Speeches, and Twitter:

    o https://www.bringthedonuts.com/
    o https://newsletter.bringthedonuts.com/
    o https://www.bringthedonuts.com/speaking/

- https://twitter.com/kennethn

Garry Tan

12. Garry Tan: President & CEO at Y Combinator, Formerly Managing Partner at Initialized Capital | Product Builder

Garry Tan is one of the leading product builders and executives in Silicon Valley today. He previously built products at various technology companies, grew his own venture firm, and now leads Y Combinator. Most if not all of his content is given away for free, and it is beneficial to almost any startup operator and product manager right now.

- Garry's Twitter and YouTube:
  - Twitter: https://twitter.com/garrytan
  - YouTube: https://www.youtube.com/c/GarryTan/videos

Julie Zhou

13. Julie Zhuo: Co-Founder @ Sundial, Author of THE MAKING OF A MANAGER, former VP Design @ FB | Product Designer & Builder

Julie Zhuo formerly led design and research at Facebook (Meta) and wrote one of the most important books on management. Julie now also works on entrepreneurial ventures and mentors emerging startup leaders. She often gives her advice for free through social media and is featured on various platforms. Any product manager should follow her for advice on how to build great products.

- Julie's Twitter and LinkedIn:
    - https://twitter.com/joulee
    - https://www.linkedin.com/in/julie-zhuo/

- *The Making of a Manager: What to Do When Everyone Looks to You:* https://www.juliezhuo.com/book/manager.html

Scott Belsky

14. Scott Belsky: Executive, Author, Investor, & Product Obsessive| Chief Product Officer at Adobe

Scott Belsky is the Chief Product Officer at Adobe as well as an author, investor, and entrepreneur. He previously founded Behance, which was acquired by Adobe. Scott often has speaking engagements and is featured on interviews. He also gives free advice to rising product and startup leaders. Scott helps connect the entrepreneurial journey with the product management career path, and he is a great model for any new or aspiring product managers.

- Scott's Twitter, LinkedIn, and Website:
    - Twitter: https://twitter.com/scottbelsky

- LinkedIn:

  https://www.linkedin.com/in/scottbelsky/

- Website: http://www.scottbelsky.com/

- *The Messy Middle: Finding Your Way Through the Hardest and Most Crucial Part of Any Bold Venture:* https://www.themessymiddle.com/

- Scott Belsky on Starting Behance, Perseverance in Business, & the "Messy Middle": Scott Belsky on Starting Behance, Perseverance in Business, & the "Messy Middle" | #AskGaryVee 290

Additional Resources For Startup Product Managers

1. YC Startup Library: https://www.ycombinator.com/library
2. How I Built This: https://wondery.com/shows/how-i-built-this/
3. Exponent is a great way to learn the basics of product management: https://www.youtube.com/c/ExponentTV/playlists
4. Talk to people who have done the job. This is the quickest way to learn about the work without necessarily doing it yet. See the previous chapter on how to write an effective cold email, which you can use to reach out to people who you are interested in networking with.

CHAPTER 14

THE ART OF PRIORITIZATION: HOW TO PRIORITIZE YOUR WORK AND MASTER YOUR TIME EFFECTIVELY AS A STARTUP PRODUCT MANAGER

Successful companies and careers are built on making decisions, working hard, creating opportunities, and trusting people. In order to accelerate your career growth and define the direction of your company, you will have to prioritize opportunities and empower your teammates to execute on these opportunities. Prioritization will be one of the most important skills for your entire career. It helps if you work efficiently towards the opportunities that you *choose* to work on. The combination of working hard and working on high-impact opportunities will define your growth trajectory as a startup product manager. Prioritization is a conscious decision to work on one opportunity over another. It is critical to prioritize effectively if you want your startup to succeed. It is also critical to prioritize effectively if you want to grow in your career. Startup product managers are paid to make the right decisions and execute well on those decisions.

"I try to prioritize in a way that generates momentum. The more I get done, the better I feel, and then the more I get done. I like to start and end each day with something I can really make progress on" — Sam Altman, CEO of OpenAI and Former President of Y-Combinator.
https://blog.samaltman.com/productivity

Your decisions, ideas, or hypotheses are facilitated through prioritization. Prioritization determines what you think of, when you think of it, and how you act on it. At a startup, you need to clearly define your priorities. Within any given period of time, there will be no deficit of work to be done. There is often a surplus of opportunities that you can work on. Startup product managers need to prioritize the right opportunities at the right time. The opportunities you need to focus are the challenging problems that will move the needle for the company and business. Within those problems, there will be a mix of exciting and monotonous tasks you need to complete. It is important to keep the top priority on top. If one project can contribute to a significant revenue increase, growth in customer satisfaction, or landing a new customer, you need to prioritize that over everything else. Prioritization can be more nuanced than this, and we will cover more on effective prioritization strategies in this chapter.

Startup product managers typically have many priorities. There may be other larger priorities that you need to juggle as a startup product manager and sub-priorities within those main priorities.

Startup product management is a game of prioritization and knowing when to solve certain problems. It also involves knowing who to trust to solve those problems. When you prioritize specific problems to solve for and solutions to execute on, you need to test your hypotheses and then turn these ideas into reality. Anyone can prioritize an idea or a solution. In order to be successful, startup product managers need to execute as well. The great startup product managers map out the execution behind their ideas and solutions. They also measure success. Ideas only work when backed by great execution and empowerment of team members. Prioritization works well when you view product management as an end to end process, which involves going from an initial idea to a successful product.

The more senior you get in your career, the responsibility you will have in the form of high-impact decision making. Working at a startup magnifies the level of responsibility that a product manager has around decision-making and prioritization. Every prioritization decision that you make as a startup product manager may either have an immediate or a downstream impact on the success of the company.

Now that we have discussed *why* prioritization is important, we will cover *how* to prioritize as a startup product manager. These are the top strategies that have worked well for me to efficiently prioritize and effectively organize my schedule as a startup product manager.

Five Effective Strategies to Prioritize as a Startup Product Manager

1. The Impact and Effort Matrix

The impact and effort matrix can be one of the most effective ways to prioritize your day. There are four quadrants to the matrix: you need to have a mix of *quick wins* and progress on *major projects*, and you need to make time for completion of *thankless tasks* and *fill-ins*.

Prioritizing by the level of impact and feasibility can help you channel your energy efficiently as a startup product manager.

The impact and effort matrix can be used to efficiently manage your day as a startup product manager. Typically, as a startup product manager, you will have back to back meetings and then blocks of time that can be used for deep work. When you go from one meeting to another, you may meet with one stakeholder and get a new request or priority that comes up. At startups, priorities are constantly shifting and changing. It is important to know that not every priority is a top priority. When possible, it helps to align on priorities with your manager to level set expectations. It also helps to take some time to step back and zoom out after talking to stakeholders, whether they are your customers or teammates. You need to remember to consciously make an effort to reevaluate the priorities that you have. It is common to keep going from one project to another, but you need to balance your time and ensure you use your energy effectively as a startup product manager. This is why the impact and effort matrix is important.

The way you can view and address your priorities is simple: work on the most important thing for that day, and after that, work on the most important things for that week. Plan out what is not urgent and what can be done later. You should also empower your team by encouraging members to take on responsibilities around execution.

2. Lists are an Essential Tool for Prioritizing

Lists are also a great way to track priorities. You can have a formal list on a tool such as Asana, an informal list on a notes app, or a simple list on pen and paper. There is no one right way to track your priorities, though it helps to consolidate your list of priorities in one location throughout the day and week. Make an effort to check in with yourself at the beginning or end of each day. Revisit, order, and prioritize the list itself over time. The goal is to have a limited list of priorities that you need to focus on. You do not need to create a never-ending to do list, as you will always have work to do. You can always create an *active* list of priorities and a *backlogged* list of priorities. The active list would be the more near-term priorities you need to address over the next month and quarter, while the backlogged list would be nice-to-haves over this period of time. This way, you can compartmentalize: you will know what you have to focus on in the near-term and long-term.

3. The Art of Saying "Yes" and "No"

Learn when to say yes, know when to say no, and understand how to delegate. The art of saying "yes" is simple: if the effort required for delivering value is worth it for the customer, the company, and your team — do it. You can always say yes to more, but equally, you need to learn how to say no. Yes, you need to ship features and ship quickly — but you need to be focused as a product manager. A lack of focus can drive you down the wrong path, and your resources will be deployed ineffectively.

The art of saying "no" is more complicated. You can use the following suggestions:

- **Listen. Understand the problem you are trying to solve.** You need to know the **context**. What is the problem, who is the customer, and what is the business impact? When you learn these facts, you can evaluate how important it is to solve these problems now. If it is not important, you do not need to do it **now**.

- **Does this solution need to come in the form of a PRD and/or user stories?** You need to ask yourself whether you need to create formal documentation around the problem and solution. Sometimes, you can solve problems through existing tools that your team has. Technology is not the only solution for a problem. You do not need to build for the sake of building. Build when you cannot solve problems through other means. If you need to build a feature, you need to validate the problem you are solving through qualitative and quantitative data. When you start to brainstorm solutions with your team and develop a hypothesis around a prioritized solution, you can write a PRD and/or user stories to help provide context for execution around the problem.

- **How does this relate to our core company objectives, ie) our North Star?** You need to understand the strategic vision of the company and the current focus areas of the business in order to be able to prioritize whether or not an opportunity makes sense to pursue in a given moment. Startup product managers can ask themselves the following questions: does this feature ultimately help our customers get to where they need to be? Does this help our mission as a company and relate to our initiatives strategically? As a startup product manager, you or founders will need to define the north star metric for your company. Almost any decision to solve a problem can relate back to the company's north star. When you define a north star metric, you can ask yourself a few more follow-up questions: what is the impact of solving a particular problem? How does solving the problem relate back to the startup's north star? What is the lift and effort required for the solution that will solve this problem? The startup's north star can help you decide *if* and *when* to build a particular feature.

- **Can we backlog this for later?** This can be an important question to ask. You do need to understand the needs of your stakeholders deeply before you start creating a solution, whether they are your customers or team members. If something is not a priority, you can backlog the request, the problem, or the idea from your stakeholders and then revisit it at a later point. You do not need to solve for every request or need right now. The team can address these items at a future time if it makes more sense to work on at a later point, in order for the team to drive customer value and stay focused. It is important to follow up with your customers and/or teammates with updates and a timeline for when it makes the most sense to move forward with an item. You can also provide an estimate for when you believe the team can make progress on this.

Further, you do not need to give an explicit "no" when you talk to a stakeholder. I would never recommend that you say "no" up front. You must listen to your stakeholders and understand their needs. You can always try to find an alternate route: you may be able to solve a problem another way, you can delegate and empower another team member, or you can often add follow-ups to your backlog to revisit later. As a startup product manager, you will need to prioritize the customer and the company first. Focus is the key to prioritization. Your decisions and priorities should be based on what will bring the most value to your customers and your company. Your judgment will be built through experience, and over time, you will learn when to yes and when to say no. Knowing the difference is the key to maintaining balance and facilitating effective prioritization as a startup product manager.

4. The Eisenhower Matrix

The Eisenhower Matrix is a simple, straightforward, and organized tool for prioritization. Startup product managers can use the matrix as a way to prioritize their days and weeks, especially when they have several different things to get done.

"Most things which are urgent are not important, and most things which are important are not urgent" — Dwight D. Eisenhower, 34th U.S. President.
https://quotefancy.com/quote/796565/Dwight-D-Eisenhower-Most-things-which-are-urgent-are-not-important-and-most-things-which

	Urgent	Not Urgent
Important	**Do** *You can do it now*	**Decide** *You can decide when to do it*
Not Important	**Delegate** *You can delegate this to someone*	**Delete** *You can delete this task*

Created by Manan Modi
Credits to Dwight D. Eisenhower

The Eisenhower Matrix helps you decide four main things: you either **do** it now, **decide** when to do it, **delegate** it to someone, or **delete** the task. This is particularly helpful when you are planning your week and have several tasks that need to be completed. If you feel overwhelmed, this is a great way to prioritize. The unique aspect of this matrix is that it clearly believes in the power of delegation. The further you get in your career as a startup product manager, you begin to understand how far you can get as a team and company if you delegate. Your mind and energy can only focus on so many things at once. Once you begin to delegate, you and your team can move quicker. Team members also feel empowered to do great work. You can also begin to focus on priorities and opportunities that need your attention and can influence the success of your startup. Over time, you can always develop your own logical thought process of prioritization. The Eisenhower Matrix is one of many matrices that can provide support in facilitating your decision-making as a startup product manager.

5. The RICE Score

The RICE Score is a great framework that helps product managers prioritize feature work and tasks. This is relevant when you have a roadmap that is very comprehensive and established, spanning across more than one quarter. The RICE score can be a great way to calculate when you should work on a feature. RICE is calculated by multiplying reach, impact, and confidence; the next step would be to divide that by effort to get the RICE score.

$$\text{RICE Score} = \frac{\text{Reach} * \text{Impact} * \text{Confidence}}{\text{Effort}}$$

- **Reach** is the the quantifiable # of people or users the feature will impact.
- **Impact** is the quantifiable impact that can be made on each user.
- **Confidence** is the quantifiable belief (confidence) that you have in the estimates you made for reach and impact.

- **Effort** is the quantifiable amount of time that it will take to accomplish this.

As a startup product manager, if you are using Asana, Excel, Sheets (or another similar software) to construct a high-level product roadmap, this framework can be especially helpful. RICE can help you quantify the value of each feature. You can automatically calculate the RICE score using the formula for each feature or task.

Granted, there are several strategies out there for prioritization. As a startup product manager, you need to find what works best for you and your team. Move fast and adapt. Your #1 priority is to provide value to your customers, solve challenging problems for them, and find ways to move the business forward for your startup. There is no one set strategy or framework that will work for everyone. You need to find what works for you.

The Impact-Effort Matrix, the Eisenhower Matrix, and the RICE score are the top three frameworks I would recommend to startup product managers to prioritize effectively. Additionally, a large fraction of the job is also being able to organize your product management schedule. The best product managers are great managers of their own schedules. We will cover effective strategies to proactively manage and organize your product management schedule.

Four Productivity Hacks to Master Your Schedule as a Startup Product Manager

"The key is not to prioritize what's on your schedule, but to schedule your priorities" — Stephen Covey, Author of The 7 Habits of Highly Effective People.
https://www.azquotes.com/quote/66166?ref=prioritize

1. Set routines and take breaks to create order in your day:

Startup product managers can have chaotic schedules. However, your ability to create order out of chaos is the very focus of the startup product management role. Product managers that thrive in chaos have been able to define a routine for themselves. The only way you navigate multiple high priorities is by handling the way you react to it. Operators set routines. In order to set effective routines and to master your schedule, you need to do an audit of your current schedule and responsibilities.

You will need to target four areas:

1. Understand the time range of your meetings during the day.
2. Categorize your meetings into two buckets: meetings you find value in and meetings you do not find value in.
3. Figure out what times you will be free (early morning, lunch, evening, and any other open time slots).

4. Find out what types of breaks you enjoy in between or after your meetings.

Startup product managers may have a set time frame when their meetings take place every week. By looking at your schedule over the previous weeks, you can understand when most of your meetings happen. You will start to identify patterns of when meetings take place and when you have free time.

Categorizing your meetings into two buckets will help you ruthlessly prioritize the meetings you need to attend or keep on your calendar. When you identify the meetings that do not provide value, you can say "no" to those meetings because it takes time away from your day to work on important tasks. Usually, there will be meetings that you can stop attending. However, some meetings may not outright provide value to you and can be informational for stakeholders. These meetings do provide value because you have an opportunity to share what the priorities are for your team and collaborate with these stakeholders. You should always reflect on your meeting schedule to check in with yourself to see if you are enjoying these meetings and if they provide value to you. Startup product managers that are particularly busy should identify opportunities to cut and reduce the time they spend in meetings that do not add value to them.

The best leaders I have seen are ones who take breaks. When you do not take time for yourself, you can often become overwhelmed and make decisions that may not be the most productive.

Startups are a marathon, not a race. You need to ensure sustainable progress over multiple years. The way to do that is to take breaks and define your balance.

Product managers are busy people, but they can definitely incorporate breaks in their day, even if they are 10 to 15 minutes or more.

- Breaks can involve cooking your favorite meal(s) of the day, walking your dog, going to the gym, driving around, spending time with your family, reading articles or a book, meditating, doing breathing exercises, playing sports, and more.
- Boundaries are hard to set, but you have to set them for yourself formally or informally. This can include doing things in the morning before you start work (listen to a podcast, go for a walk), setting a time when you start, creating to-do lists and adding to them throughout the week (focusing only on the highest priority items first), blocking out the time you have for lunch, setting a time when you stop, or going for a walk after work.

In order to make progress, startup product managers need to be intentional about when they do things. There are times when you need to communicate with your team and stakeholders, and there are times when you need to do heads down work to move projects forward. One way to help others understand your schedule and the work you need to get done is by creating a schedule that includes meeting blocks.

2. Create meeting blocks on your calendar to help you do deep and focused work:

As a startup product manager, you need to create time to do **deep and focused work**. It is important to establish when your meetings will be and when your meetings will not be. As mentioned before, you need to create order in your schedule as a startup product manager.

You can *formally* create blocks on your calendar. Alternatively you can *informally* tell yourself that, during certain periods of time, you will focus on XYZ. You *need* to make time either for formally or informally doing work.

If you are finding that you have no time, you can create a **"no meeting"** block on your calendar. This will tell everyone that schedules a meeting with you when to schedule and when not to schedule a meeting. Startup product managers are meant to prioritize and use their time efficiently to identify, as well as execute on, opportunities that will help customers and the broader business. You can manage your time more effectively by creating no meeting blocks. In an increasingly remote work environment, you need to signal to your team members when you are unavailable and when you do not want to take meetings.

These are the times that can be perfect for doing other work or taking breaks.

Here are a few suggestions:

- **West Coast Product Managers:** you can create "no meeting" blocks during early mornings. Further, you can also propose new times for meetings with your stakeholders and try to avoid meetings that are too early for you. Later in the day, it may also make sense to do focused work because that is when your East Coast and international teammates are starting to log off. *Note: If you have team members based on the east coast, they may be eating lunch around 12:00 or 1:00 p.m. (which is 9:00 a.m. or 10:00 a.m. your time).*

- **East Coast Product Managers:** you can create "no meeting" blocks after 3-4 p.m. onwards if your team meets primarily in the morning. Generally, you can also schedule most of your meetings in the morning or even propose times to your stakeholders to meet earlier in the day. If your team is primarily on the west coast, you will naturally have more time earlier in the mornings and instead may have meetings later in the morning and into the afternoon. *Note: If you have team members based on the west coast, they may be eating lunch around 12:00 or 1:00 p.m. (which is 3:00 p.m. or 4:00 p.m. your time).*

Note: you will have to adapt your schedule based on whether you have team members working internationally as well.

3. Snooze notifications, define a level of balance for yourself, and set boundaries:

A great way to boost your productivity is to create balance for yourself. One way to create balance for yourself is to snooze notifications after certain hours or on the weekends. Sometimes you also have to just keep your phone away, so you do not keep checking it and become obsessed with work. One of the worst things to happen to a startup product manager is burnout, so knowing what your limits are and actively managing how much time you spend on your job will help you maintain your productivity over a longer period of time. As mentioned before, startups are a marathon and not a race.

Balance is different from person to person, but you can consider turning off Slack (or other communication platforms) after a certain time. You can repurpose this for other tools, such as Microsoft Teams.

Most startups and tech companies use Slack. Snooze your notifications when you are not working. You do not need to be online past a certain time, say 7:30 pm. Use your judgment and know when it is important to respond and when it can wait. Especially if you are new to startups or product management, you *need* to set boundaries. What matters is working efficiently and effectively, as well as delivering an impact. You need a consistent and prolonged effort within a reasonable number of hours a day in order to achieve what you want to achieve at work.

3. Great startup product managers play like point guards in basketball:

We can use a basketball analogy to describe your role as a product manager at a startup. Point guards in basketball usually play 48 minutes per game. Whether you score 20 points and land 10 assists within 48 minutes in a regular game or within 60 minutes in an overtime game, you still had the same impact. No point guard can consistently play 60 minute games every day, drive an impact for their team, and still win games. They need to rest and take breaks. Whether you win a game in 30 minutes or 48 minutes, you still won the game. Having an impact and being the best team player you can be, to achieve the objectives you hope to achieve, are what matters in startups.

Startup product managers are like point guards. Startup product managers similarly need to manage their pace, understand which problems are the right problems to solve, know how to solve problems, build trust with their teams, and learn how to work well with others. It is about balancing the quality of work for the quantity of work that you produce. Startup product managers build businesses, and no business was built in one day. Businesses are built through concerted team efforts over months and years.

Startup product managers need to maintain a proper pace and balance over their schedule and time. In order to successfully play the role of a product manager at a startup, you have to be the point-guard of your game.

CHAPTER 15

THE BLUEPRINT TO BUILDING: HOW TO WRITE GREAT USER STORIES THAT EMPOWER YOUR TEAMS

User stories are the building blocks that help teams create products. They help startup product managers communicate their vision into its fundamental, encompassing parts. These building blocks are what help your teams execute on the vision and decide how to build what you are envisioning. Startup product managers will take on the role of writing user stories at a startup at one point or another in their career. I want to provide a framework for writing great user stories as a startup product manager. User stories are the language you use to communicate with your design and engineering teams.

Later on, I will present a user story that will solve a problem for a product that you know about: TikTok.

Writing great user stories makes your teams stronger and feel more invested. Organizations have their product or engineering teams write user stories. It is an important skill to know, so that you can be adaptable to any startup or company that you go to. And if you decide to become a founder one day, it will be immensely valuable to set a stellar foundation for product execution.

To preface, I think that many teams across many companies require that product managers write stories. Writing stories can be a valuable learning experience, but I do not think they are a necessary responsibility for product managers alone. There are other team members who can take on this responsibility. Startup product managers should know how to wear multiple hats, which can involve writing user stories. However, in order to progress your career, you should focus more time on users and the business in order to drive the most impact for your company. Knowing how to write stories and learning to empower others to do so are both critical to building products.

The core takeaway from this chapter is knowing that while writing user stories can be an important part of your toolkit, it is not the only way to do things. Product managers do not have to write user stories. At some companies, user stories do not exist. It is important for product managers to focus on alignment and context around the problem first. Next, it is about driving the right solution. User stories are merely one of many mediums to achieve this. There are successful teams and companies where product managers do not write stories directly. They are still able to generate great outcomes. Your job as a product manager is to communicate the context to your engineers, designers, marketers, and more. You need to know *why* you are solving a particular problem and be able to paint the vision behind that.

The Six Components of a Great User Story

1. What makes a great user story?

After reading several articles and learning from different product managers, I want to tell you about a few core principles that can make a user story great. This framework can give you the foundation to write user stories that empower your teams.

1. **Focus on the customer problem.** Who are these customers? What problem are your customers facing?
2. **Tell a story (add context).** Why solve this problem now?
3. **Talk about why it's important for the bigger picture strategy (optional, can be part of PRDs).** What is the impact of solving this problem? How does it impact overall product strategy, revenue, and growth?
4. **Paint the picture.** How will you solve these problems? You can attach a link to your design concept, from Figma, if applicable. You can add clarity and context to your Figma files by including helper text or by talking through your designs with your teams.
5. **Write clearly. Write succinctly.** Only write as much as you feel you need to. Default to keeping it simple and to the point.
6. **Empower your teams to execute**. Trust your team to execute and give them the context to do so. Startup product managers should enable them to solve problems

in the way they can. You do not need to write or outline everything for them.

When you are going over user stories, you should focus on the problem the end user is having and the vision you have for the solution. People learn through hearing, visuals, and reading. They **read** the user story. You must go over the design in Figma **visually** and walk through it with the engineering. You must **talk** through and allow them to **hear** the surrounding context, the value of the problem you are solving, and why this is important for the customer. The engineering team should be empowered to determine execution.

The Two Foundational Secrets of a Great User Story

1. Start with the problem and business context before writing a user story:

We can start with our example of TikTok that I mentioned before. **Note:** this level of detail may be included in a product-requirements document, but you can summarize it within a user story if needed. Also, the level of detail you provide for your user persona can vary.

1. **Hypothetical problem:** TikTok users often use the search feature to find fun outdoor activities to do (places to visit, food to eat, etc), so that they can find exciting activities in their city to engage in with friends. However, they cannot

do this well right now because: 1) they are unsure how the searches are often ordered, 2) they sometimes find irrelevant content when they are looking.

2. **Business Context:** We can say that 1 in every 5 TikTok users engages with the search feature to find fun outdoor activities, such as finding places to visit and food to eat. That is over 360 million users. That is the level of impact that solving this problem can have. In the future, we can entice creators to create content in these niches, monetize active users that watch this content by strategically targeting ads for power users, and more.

How to Write a Great User Story: A Guided Example

3. How to write a great user story:

User stories typically model the jobs to be done framework that was popularized by Tony Ulwick:

When I ____ , I want to ____ , so I can ____

Situation   Motivation   Expected Outcome

Created by Manan Modi
Credits to Tony Ulwick

User Story Format: As a __, I want to ___, so that I can ___.

- As a [type of user], I want to [action the user takes], so that I can [the why, impact, and context].

User Story Example With Acceptance Criteria

Now, using these learnings, we can write a user story based on the TikTok scenario we mentioned earlier.

User Story: As a TikTok watcher, I want to use the search feature to find categorical recommendations for outdoor activities in my city (such as places to visit, food to eat), so that I can quickly find the top things to do in my free time with my friends.

This is important [**insert why it is valuable**] because over 1 in 5 TikTok users engage with the search feature to find fun outdoor activities in their city. However, they cannot do this well right now because: 1) they are unsure how the searches are often ordered, 2) they sometimes find irrelevant content when they are looking. By solving this problem, we can order searches in a more organized way.

Insert Design (Figma) link here: www.figma.com/....

- *These are any screens that your designers have created and will be used by your engineers.*

Acceptance Criteria (MVP):

- TikTok users can see categorical recommendations for places to visit by type of activity when they search for "top things to do in [insert city]" (Concerts, Sports, Comedy, etc).
- TikTok users can see categorical recommendations for types of food to eat when they search for "top food to eat in [insert city]" (Mexican, Italian, Thai, etc)
- TikTok users can save categories when they search and create collections using these categories — similar to how they save videos that are on their for you pages.
- TikTok users can share categorical recommendations that they find exciting with their friends.

I also want to say that your user stories do not need to be as long as this. This can be helpful in surrounding context for a PRD as well. When you are writing several stories, you simply may not have the time to write this level of context every time. You can always create a briefer or shorter user story.

Writing For Frontend Versus Backend Developers

You can split up your stories into two buckets: frontend and backend tickets. Depending on how you work with your engineering teams, you can adapt the strategy mentioned next. If you are ever writing user stories, you can do the following:

- **Frontend user stories:** your frontend tickets can mimic your design (similar to the user story I wrote above). The frontend tickets will typically come more naturally to startup product managers because it is straightforward. You primarily review your design concepts and think through the requirements that are needed to implement that design.

- **Backend user stories:** when you do not have an engineering manager, you may need to write the backend tickets. Your ability to write backend tickets is built through communicating with your backend developers. You can always ask your backend developer for help on what they would like to see.

With enough repetition, you will see the patterns and be able to anticipate what a frontend story entails versus what a backend story entails.

As mentioned, every startup and every company does this differently. Product managers do not always have to write user stories. Engineering may also write user stories. Sometimes, a startup may not even have the process of writing user stories. Whether you write user stories or not does not matter, but what matters is that there is a structured and seamless way for your teams to build effectively. The important takeaway for this chapter is that your teams feel invested in the end product they build. They will do the work that is necessary to implement a feature, and startup product managers are responsible for communicating the context and requirements clearly. When startup product managers write user stories, it is especially important that you focus on the context: the **problem**, the **customer**, and **why** it is important to solve a problem. When you build trust with your teams, they will figure out **how** to best solve a problem. Building products is a cross-functional process between product managers and their teammates. Everyone has to play their part in creating the right *environment* in order to build the right *products.*

CHAPTER 16

THE TWO PRODUCT MANAGEMENT TEAM STRATEGIES YOU NEED TO KNOW ABOUT

There are traditionally two forms of product management teams that exist: Waterfall and Agile. At a startup, you will likely use one of these methodologies in order to build products as a team. Processes **do not** define how you build products. Processes should instead augment or supplement how you build products. Startup product managers should keep in mind that the goal is to create structure and not red-tape. More formal processes are not necessarily a good thing when you are trying to move quickly. There is no right answer to adopting one process or another, but it is important to create awareness of both types of methodologies for product management.

"Coming together is a beginning, staying together is progress, and working together is success" — Henry Ford.
https://blog.hubspot.com/marketing/teamwork-quotes

It is a distinction that all product managers should understand — it can significantly affect your growth, trajectory, responsibilities, and satisfaction. There are great lessons to be learned from both Waterfall and Agile.

Why The Waterfall Versus Agile Distinction is Crucial For Product Managers

1. Why the Waterfall and Agile Distinction is Important for Product Managers:

Knowing the difference between Waterfall and Agile teams will have a huge impact in your role as a Product Manager. From my experience, the two methodologies are equally valuable: there are pros and cons to each. Teams usually fall into either bucket, or they take a mix of principles from each. The best teams are flexible to adapting. There are important distinctions between Waterfall teams and Agile teams. Having overseen the transition from a Waterfall to an Agile environment, I have directly seen how the product management role can evolve and change over time. Understanding the difference between these two processes is absolutely critical to know because it affects your growth, your responsibilities, your interactions in your day to day job, your goals, and more. The most important difference between Agile and Waterfall methodologies is **what** you spend your time on.

The earlier you are in your product management career, the more valuable it can be for you to start out as a generalist. You want to be exposed to different forms of product management and interact with as many teams as you can early on. If you join a startup, your goals likely involve optimizing for learning and career growth. You also should learn everything you can about the product management function and role. As you get more senior, you may want to specialize in certain aspects of the role. This is where it is critical to know the difference between Agile and Waterfall. It will help you understand what your day to day work will entail. It is important to remember that teams can be highly adaptable. There is no right or wrong way to define a culture or team by its methodology. What works well for one team may not work well for another team.

As mentioned, product teams typically fall into a bucket: Waterfall or Agile. Product Managers typically have an overlap of responsibilities between both types of teams. However, time is limited as a product manager at a startup especially. The difference comes in what they get to **focus** on day to day. This is what delivers your growth and satisfaction as a PM.

What is Waterfall? The Top Pros And Cons

3. What is Waterfall?

Waterfall is a more sequential process. Waterfall consists of 5 main stages in the product development processes: requirements, design, implementation, verification, and maintenance. Some of the top startups and big tech companies use Waterfall today. It is the most tried and true methodology in tech, and it has proven to be successful over and over again.

Product managers here typically focus more on discovery, talking to customers, owning the roadmap, writing requirements, talking to business units, analyzing metrics, interacting more frequently with design, and aligning with engineering on requirements. They focus less on running and having oversight over the implementation phase, which involves executing over designs. Waterfall naturally leads to product managers focusing on the earlier stages of product development. Engineering has greater influence and autonomy over execution of designs. Modern Waterfall includes a greater customer focus for the product management role.

In Waterfall environments, engineering managers and engineers primarily write user stories. There may also be product owners who write requirements for engineering. At larger companies, you may see product owners on teams. Product managers typically do not write as many user stories for engineering. This is the largest distinction between Waterfall and Agile, but it does not apply to necessarily all teams. In Agile, which we will cover more later, product managers have more ownership over engineering execution. In Waterfall, product managers focus more on the beginnings of the product development process: customer discovery, writing requirements, working with design, aligning with engineering once designs are ready, validating what gets shipped, measuring success and failure, and more. Agile does this to an extent too, but from my experience, there is more of a focus on these stages within Waterfall teams. Agile *can* focus on those stages as well, but product managers simply do not have time for everything. As a result, the time that product managers spend writing requirements and tickets for engineering can often take time away from working on other areas. In Waterfall, engineers or product owners further own the process of writing stories as well as what proceeds after. They are also involved in planning technical sprints, testing features before launch, validating features, and maintaining features. When looking at Waterfall, there are several pros and cons we can use to evaluate the methodology for product managers.

Pros:

- As a product manager, you can focus more on discovery and market research. You spend more time talking to customers, understanding the key metrics more, and evaluating more strategically where the company is headed.

- Waterfall product managers may have more siloed and focused responsibilities because they do not necessarily have to own the end to end process of product development. As a result, they can focus significantly more on the early parts of the product development process and still have interaction on the execution side with design and engineering. You will not have to focus as much on writing stories or have to plan engineering sprints.

- You may have more time to interact with business teams and focus on strategic work if you are comfortable with execution. Engineers and product owners are empowered to write tasks in Waterfall, so there may be a more even split of responsibilities. I suggest for many senior product managers and beyond that Waterfall teams will better suit your career growth. It ultimately comes down to what you value and whether you want to focus more on customer problems and the business **or** solving complex technical problems. If you prefer the former, you may find that Waterfall is better suited for your interests. If you prefer the latter, you may find that Agile is better suited for your interests.

Cons:

- As a startup product manager, you may not have as much time to focus on engineering-related execution on a Waterfall team. You may not write as many user stories or work with QA. Engineering naturally would have the most oversight over any implementation and execution. The role may be less technical by nature.
- If you are an associate product manager or if this is your first product management role, you may not fully see what working with engineering fully looks like unless you have been in an engineering role. You also may be building products without having the experience or intuition yet to

know the technical lift and effort required to build features. However, as you get more senior and understand execution, you may want to focus naturally on discovery and strategic work. Waterfall allows you to focus more on discovery and strategic work, but this may come at the cost of making more engineering decisions and mastering your craft of technical execution.

- The team structure of Waterfall can feel segmented. There are opportunities here for the team to become more agile and empower team members to take on cross-team responsibilities to decrease the level of segmentation. Everyone has a "process" that they own on Waterfall teams. Product managers talk to customers and define requirements. Designers create concepts for these requirements. Product managers review the concepts and requirements, and next, they get sign off from engineering. Product managers hand off concepts to engineering, and engineering handles implementation. Engineers or designers may not be in constant communication with product managers from the inception of every idea or feature that gets created. Further, there may be less of a sprint concept that is spearheaded by product management on Waterfall teams. Engineering may have their own sprints that they lead based on the designs and requirements that are handed off to them. Product managers have to make an effort to check in with design and engineering to deliver that context. Otherwise, communication can break down and features may not be built correctly. Experience and communication helps ensure this does not happen. As a product manager, you have to be more proactive about checking in on processes you do not necessarily own on Waterfall teams.

What is Agile? The Top Pros And Cons

4. What is Agile?

Agile is newer by nature. Agile product management has been touted as the methodology that teams are considering more recently. Waterfall, however, still remains a successful approach at many successful startups and large tech companies. Ultimately, having tried both, Agile and Waterfall have their own pros and cons.

Agile can be considered a more all-encompassing approach to building products. The segmentation of stages we covered in Waterfall is more of a cohesive process in Agile, which is cyclical in nature and owned by product management. Product managers have more control over every process of product development: requirements, design, implementation, testing, and maintenance. It can be considered a more iterative process, in which product managers closely plan sprints with engineering team members and have a lot more oversight into the execution. There are upsides and downsides to working on Agile teams. Product managers on Agile teams have a more end to end view of product development. However, given that time is limited, they have to prioritize where they focus their energy a bit more. As a result, they may not necessarily have time to do everything "strategic." The product management role can be very executional in nature on Agile teams.

Pros:

- Agile allows product managers to get a lens into execution with engineering. You are writing user stories and working almost daily with design and engineering. Generally, your responsibilities are much more varied.
- You have to wear multiple hats. This is a pro and con. Your teams may be more empowered because you have to communicate and work with your teams from ideation to full implementation. Product, design, and engineering teams may be more cross-functional as a result.
- If you want to be a founder one day, you should grow your knowledge of different team structures: whether it is Agile or Waterfall. Knowing how all these different processes work can be valuable. At the end of the day, you get to choose. You can choose whether you want Waterfall or Agile, have a mix of both, or define a new structure and cadence for your team.

- You learn to filter a lot. You manage the roadmap, as well as taking in feature requests and balancing bugs and tech debt. You learn when to say yes, as well as when to say no.

Cons:

- Agile product managers can have more varied responsibilities, and this can require a large time commitment. You are responsible for end to end product development, from ideation to implementation. You will not have time to do everything as a product manager on an Agile team. This can result in more responsibilities overall for a product manager because they have to influence and execute even more across teams. This can become overwhelming, and it may be more difficult to specialize in a particular type of work as a functional generalist.

- Product management roles on Agile teams can teach you how to execute and implement ideas with engineering teams at a very granular level, but it can involve working on less strategic initiatives in terms of focusing your time on the business and customers. Given your time is limited, you have to make tradeoffs: you might need to focus more on engineering execution versus on customer discovery. On Agile teams, product managers have to make an intentional effort in dedicating time to customer discovery: talking to customers, prioritizing problems to solve, brainstorming solutions, and more. Without an active effort in doing so, you will naturally focus on other aspects of product development and not have the time to do customer discovery.

- In theory, Agile teams are built on continuous discovery by talking to customers. However, in practice, you will not have as much time to do that consistently as a product manager on Agile teams while also planning sprints and writing user stories. However, to become great at developing strategy you must understand what good execution looks like. Product managers should work on Agile teams to understand execution, but in order to focus more on upfront research and ideation, product managers should work on Waterfall teams.

- Product managers on Agile teams are the filter through which the team takes feature requests as well as bugs and tech debt. Waterfall product managers mainly focus on feature requests, but Agile product managers need to do much more. You will learn a lot on Agile teams by balancing bugs and tech debt. This provides a more holistic view on optimizing the product as well, but it can feel repetitive to write tickets to solve bugs and prioritize tech debt. The upside is that it helps you become better at prioritization: it can help you a lot as a founder when you run your own business or as the head of product if you lead a product team one day. Founders and those who lead the product always need to test out the product, determine ways to make it better, and identify any bugs before their customers do.

- You also may have less time to interact with business stakeholders from a strategic standpoint, such as working on the go-to-market strategy of a feature launch. Naturally, product managers on Agile teams are focused on planning the current sprint, strategizing the next sprint, and writing stories for future sprints. Product managers may have to take more ownership of responsibilities if engineers are not empowered to run sprint planning and writing user stories.

- You may have less involvement from an ideation and design standpoint than you would in a Waterfall environment. If you are naturally a design-focused product manager, Waterfall teams may not suit you as much, but if you are a technical product manager, they may be a better fit. Granted, there is no one "label" that defines you as a product manager: all of these skills are valuable. It is more about what you enjoy doing and then making time for that.

Both methodologies can be appreciated for the unique challenges and responsibilities they provide for product managers. Teams can vary in how they adopt each methodology. There is no one right or wrong way. Often, the best methodology is the unique structure and foundation that your own team creates using their own experiences as well as insights. Product management, especially at startups, can vary from company to company. But **knowing** how each methodology applies to the product management role is critical to understand because you can adapt learnings from both in practice. The methodologies are a starting point, but it is more about your team's ability to form its own identity. The mindset your team adopts can have a significant impact on how you solve problems and build great products. A culture of adaptation, continuous learning, communication, and openness are what will help you build a successful startup and product management team.

CHAPTER 17

TOP COMPENSATION SECRETS FOR PRODUCT MANAGERS

Compensation is one of the most exciting and challenging topics to talk about as a product manager. At startups, there is not a clearly defined title progression or compensation progression for product managers. This is often because there have not been fully-constructed product teams and processes around this, but this allows for more opportunity for you to move up quicker or find higher compensation if that is what you desire. This chapter will focus on demystifying all of the secrets around compensation in order to help you negotiate effectively in compensation discussions as a product manager, whether you are at a startup or larger company.

"In negotiations, "win-win is a belief in the Third Alternative. It's not your way or my way; it's a better way, a higher way" — Stephen Covey, Author of The 7 Habits of Highly Effective People. *https://quotefancy.com/quote/909527/Stephen-R-Covey-Win-win-is-a-belief-in-the-Third-Alternative-It-s-not-your-way-or-my-way*

Learning how to negotiate your compensation well comes through experience, as well as trial and error. These are the most important lessons I have learned about negotiating compensation.

The Keys to Understanding Your Pay Structure

1. The Higher-Level Principles of Compensation:

Interviewing is half of the process. Negotiation is the other half. In order to have the right context for negotiation, you need to know how your compensation will be structured. We will focus on two core parts of compensation: salary and equity.

The Strategy to Negotiating Your Salary as a PM

2. Salary:

Compensation typically consists of salary, equity, and benefits. These numbers are always negotiable. There are also additional factors that can play a role such as a bonus (quarterly or annual), sign-on bonuses, and promotion cycles.

Salary can be understood through knowing the compensation "band" of a role. When you ask a recruiter about the compensation band of a role, they will likely provide you with a range of numbers where you can expect your salary to be. You can essentially get the compensation range of any role without you giving a number first.

Never give a number first. When you do this, recruiters will also know that you have done your homework. You need to understand the compensation band for every product role that you look for.

- You can ask: "What is the compensation band that is currently being offered for this role?"
- Recruiter: "Our budget for this role is $120k to $140k base. Our hiring manager can provide additional details on equity and other benefits."

Your previous compensation should not hinder or prevent you from getting a role. It is often recommended that you **do not** give your current salary or total compensation before they tell you a number. You should ask as many questions as possible to gain context into what the company is willing to offer you.

As mentioned in the video below, **do your research**. Know what other companies are offering at the role or level you are at. Here are a few great resources:

- Startup Salary & Equity Database: https://topstartups.io/startup-salary-equity-database
- Levels.fyi

If you do get to the offer stage for a product management role, you can choose to optimize for salary over equity (or equity over salary). I created a due diligence playbook to evaluate startups to join when you are making this decision. Please feel free to go to an earlier chapter to see this.

More salary over equity can be an option in compensation discussions for product management roles. It all depends on overall risk tolerance, liquidity goals, and startup trajectory. Negotiating for more salary is typically better and can be a hedge for risk, as startup equity is inherently risky given that 90% of startups fail. Startup equity is illiquid, and it can take years for you to exit or sell your shares. If this product role is not my first or second job, if I have savings, and if I do not have major debt/liabilities, I would potentially consider taking on more equity. Typically I prefer to take on more salary than equity, but it all depends on the opportunity being presented. If I can afford to take on risk, I would go for more equity if I felt comfortable financially. These learnings are based on prior experiences, and you ultimately decide the compensation structure. This is what I would do, but you can always choose to take a different approach. We will dive deeper into equity in the next section.

Why Equity is Important For Your Long-Term Career Success

3. Equity

It is important to know how your equity compensation will be structured. Equity compensation is important because you can one day have a financially vested interest in the company you work for. After a period of time, you can usually own part of the startup. You can even continue to own this equity after you have left the company. If the startup continues to grow over time and raise higher valuations, your startup equity in principle will be valued higher. Salary compensation is often capped, and you might have a pay increase every year. You might have a bonus. Hence, the *might*. Your equity from any startup can go to zero or be worth significantly more than the value you got it for. There is no set value for what equity may be worth after a period of time. Salary may help you get rich, but owning equity in companies is the key to building wealth. Owning startup equity can be life changing for many people.

The Strategy to Negotiating Your Stock Options as a Product Manager

4. Stock Options

At a minimum, you should understand the following about your equity: how much equity is being offered for a position, the vesting schedule, the total number of outstanding shares, the percentage of the company you would own, the strike price per share, the exercise price per share, and the expected stock price.

- You may ask: "How much equity is being offered for this position?"
- Recruiter says: "We are offering 35,000 shares for this role."

- You ask: "How many total outstanding shares have been issued by the company?"
- Recruiter says: "15,000,000 shares have been issued."
- You ask: "Will I receive RSUs or Stock Options? What is the strike price?"
- Recruiter says: "You will receive 35,000 options over 4 years. The strike price would be $0.25 per share."
- You ask: "What is the vesting schedule?"
- Recruiter says: "We have a standard four-year vesting schedule. After your first year, 25% of your shares will vest. You will be provided the option to purchase 8,750 shares. Every month after that, you will have the option to purchase approximately 729 shares additionally." (35,000– 0.25*35,000)/36 = 729...

Knowing this information, you can estimate how much options can be worth. Assuming you are at a Series A startup, you **can** own approximately 0.23% of the company if you have the option to purchase 35,000 shares out of 15,000,000 outstanding shares (35,000/15,000,000). If the company is valued at $100 million, those fully vested shares would have a theoretical total value of $230,000 at the current valuation. With the current vesting structure, you would have the opportunity to purchase ¼ of total shares every year. After your first year, you get the chance to exercise a fraction of total options every month for your remaining time. This assumes that the shares can be sold and that the private markets continue to value the company at that valuation. It is important to note that there can be down-rounds or up-rounds. The valuation of the startup, if it can raise another round, can change over time. If we take the numbers from the scenario mentioned earlier, we can estimate the value you can gain per share of the company you own.

- The **stock price** per share, right now, would be estimated at $6.57 per share.
- As mentioned, the **strike or exercise price** would be $0.25 per share.
- The **difference** between the stock price and strike price = $6.57 - $0.25 = $6.32 before taxes.

The strike price is the price you would pay for those shares. The stock price is the current value of those shares. You would subtract the strike price from the stock price. The difference between the stock price and strike price would be the approximate profit per share, not including taxes. In this scenario, you can have a private market profit of $6.32 per share prior to taxes. There are a few things to note.

- There can be dilution. This means more shares can be issued over time, and resultantly, your percentage ownership can go down. Typically, this happens at a higher valuation at a future round. Sometimes, there are down rounds during a recession where companies raise more capital at a lower valuation. The value of your shares should go up over time, but the percentage of the company you "own" will typically go down.

- Further, your shares will be private. Assume that it will take 8 to 10 years for the company to go public. *See https://lao.ca.gov/LAOEconTax/Article/Detail/685*

- Your shares can be sold in secondary markets if you decide to sell them earlier. Companies such as EquityZen allow you to sell your shares in the private market, but likely, these shares must be sold at a discount. Secondary markets such as EquityZen also have restrictions on the types of shares you can sell and the companies they accept on their markets for buying or selling shares.

- If you need liquidity, you can also contact current investors if they would like to buy your shares. If the shares are high in demand, you can get a comparable deal to traditional secondary markets. Typically, however, when you go to investors you may have to sell your shares at a discount unless you offer shares for a startup they are truly looking for.

- You may have the option of exercising your options early — "early exercise." You could hypothetically buy your shares before the vesting date if your company allows it. *See https://www.investopedia.com/terms/e/earlyexercise.asp*

- About 65% of Series A startups get a Series B funding round, which can allow them to keep going. However, 35% of Series A startups fail. It is important to know that your options can go to 0. You need to take an objective look at the market and how the market values your startup. You may know the trajectory of your startup, but the external perception of your startup will often help you value your startup shares. Ultimately, you and those at your startup will know the trajectory of your startup better than anyone. You can consult venture capitalists or other startup operators for advice. However, it is your decision to make if you want to exercise your options - as well as when to buy or sell shares of a startup.

- As mentioned, your shares can also devalue over time if the startup raises money at a lower valuation in environments where capital is tight and funding is needed to ensure the survivability of the startup.

- Index Ventures Options Calculator: https://www.indexventures.com/optionplan/#expected_fu nding_rounds_pre_exit=series-b-and- c&employee_country=us&mode=seed

Why Restricted Stock Units (RSUs) Are a Unique Form of Equity Compensation

5. Restricted Stock Units (RSUs)

You can also receive RSUs instead of Stock Options. This happens notably at public companies and later stage startups. You will likely have a similar vesting schedule: 25% after the first year and then 1/36 every month onwards. However, you will not have to pay a strike price. You will receive the shares without purchasing them. This is a key benefit of RSUs. You will need to pay taxes when you sell those RSUs. The downside of this is that your shares can be valued highly when you join, but if the valuation of the company goes down, your share price will go down as well. RSUs are primarily different from options in that you do not have to pay for or exercise RSUs. Once these shares vest, you can get these shares without additional payment.

The Top Resources For Negotiating Compensation as a Product Manager

6. The Best Compensation Resources for PMs

These educational resources can help you build on what we covered earlier in the chapter. They will help you become the best advocate and negotiator for yourself and your career as a product manager. All of these resources can be found on YouTube.

a. *How to Negotiate Your Tech Salary Simulation:* This video by Exponent and Levels.fyi will provide a simulation of how to negotiate your salary to your advantage. I **highly** recommend you watch this video before you go into interviewing or negotiating.
How to Negotiate Your Tech Salary Simulation ft. Levels.fyi

b. *Everything I Learned to Negotiate Your Salary:* This video will give you the best and quick overview of compensation at tech companies, specifically tailored for product managers. Everything I Learned to Negotiate Your Salary 🦑 🦑

c. *Chris Voss — 3 Tips on Negotiations, with FBI Negotiator:* Chris Voss is a former FBI Negotiator and the CEO & Founder of the Black Swan Group. If you want to understand negotiation, he is one of the best teachers of it. These tips are highly translatable not only for compensation discussions but also for your day to day life. Chris Voss - 3 Tips on Negotiations, with FBI Negotiator

The Best Compensation Advice I Have Received

7. The Best Compensation Advice I Have Received

"If you are at an early stage company, you should focus **less** on [the following]: "how do I get promoted, or how do I get a raise?" You should focus **more** on "how do I best make the company succeed?" – Jackie Bavaro
Source: Lenny's Product Management Fundamentals Course

Yes, compensation matters. How much you get paid will be very important in your career. It can determine how quickly you can pay off debt, build wealth, retire early, plan your kids' education, and more. In short, it can help you meet your financial and any personal goals.

The mindset you can adopt as a product manager is to optimize for compensation **before** you join the company and establish a plan with your manager to continue growing at the company. **After** you join the company, your main goal should be trying to determine how to make the company succeed and how to continue growing in your career. When joining a startup, the main objective should not be to play the compensation game early on in your career. An extra 10k, 20k, 30k can add up, but you typically join a startup for other reasons. You join an early stage company for the **learning** and **meaningful equity** that comes with it. Remember, you can always negotiate. The most effective times to negotiate are before you join the company and when you are nearing a review cycle. There is less structure at startups, so if you feel like your impact and value warrants more recognition, you can advocate for yourself at any time.

Keep the main thing the main thing. The goal of a startup is to help it succeed and help yourself grow, and when you focus less on the material goals for yourself, you will likely achieve more when you focus more of your brainpower on the company and customers. Do not be afraid to be selfish and to advocate for your career, but you need to balance it with your broader goals. Keep that in balance with your **why** and your reasons for joining a startup versus working for a larger company.

The Top Compensation Advice I Give to Others

7. The Top Compensation Advice I Give to Others

- I advise you to optimize your growth for your first startup product management role. Your learning will compound. Join a company for the learning, the values, and the mission. When you switch companies, ideally, your total compensation is higher than your previous company. Salary is important. But you should not be concerned about waiting the first year out for your equity to vest, especially when they are stock options and can go to zero. Do not focus your free time on calculating the probability of how much your equity will be worth at a future round if things go according to plan. Nothing will go 100% according to plan.

- If you want to "optimize" your compensation, there is a way to do that. A good company will value you and recognize you, though you always have that option to switch companies when you feel comfortable. You do need to advocate for yourself internally by sharing projects and impact with higher ups. As a startup product manager, you need to be the most helpful person at the company. Be that person who provides value to others, and you will become irreplaceable. If you are at a startup and feel undervalued, likely, it can be difficult to get a raise within the first 6 months or even a year sometimes — even if you are crushing it. It is not impossible, however. If you are worried about your compensation, you can switch jobs. Most people get raises through switching, not through staying at the same company.

- Respect yourself first. Recognition is earned, not given. When you deliver an impact and advocate for yourself, you have done the hard work. Succeeding at a startup is not easy, and you need to build the confidence and comfortability in letting people know about the impact you made. You should have respect for yourself by recognizing that your startup needs to reciprocate that sentiment. If a startup does not recognize you, after you perform time and time again, you need to reevaluate whether it is the right company for you to be at. Great managers will continue to advocate for you behind the scenes, and great companies will recognize its top performers and keep them happy. To build any great company, executives know that they need to support and reinvest into talent to continue building a culture that supports growth as well as retention.

- If you do not believe in your startup equity's value in terms of what it could be worth and are looking for a raise, you should reconsider the company you are at. It is okay to take a pay cut if this is your first job or first startup product manager role. Likely, if you keep at it, you will find another product management role and company that you want to stay at long term within a year. You should **not** come in with the mentality of the following: *how do I maximize my equity or compensation at this company?* Those are questions you should answer **before** you join the company.

At the end of the day, you know your value. You know what you are capable of. Every role or stage of your career is a stepping stone to the next.

CHAPTER 18

THE TOP TEN LIST OF POWERFUL HABITS FOR PRODUCT MANAGERS

The habits that you set in your first 30 days as a startup product manager will significantly affect how you get to influence and grow throughout the time you are at a startup. Habits set first impressions, habits allow you to influence without authority, and habits help you deliver outcomes. The first 30 days are key to your success and acceleration on the job. This chapter will provide you with a step by step guide on how to navigate your first 30 days as a product manager. These are strategies that will help you throughout your career, at any company.

"If you get one percent better each day for one year, you'll end up thirty-seven times better by the time you're done" — James Clear, Author of Atomic Habits.
https://jamesclear.com/continuous-improvement

Why Habits Help Startups And Product Managers Achieve Success

Why Building Habits Will Help You as a Startup Product Manager

Startups are chaotic and exciting. As a startup product manager, your ability to navigate the chaos by building concrete habits will help you thrive in this environment and create a form of normalcy.

It can be stressful being a new startup product manager. You may feel overwhelmed going into your first full-time startup product management role. You also might be starting your second, third, or fourth product management role. Every role is different, and you **will** become better after each one. These habits are lessons that new or experienced product managers can apply to their first few months on the job and help them quickly acclimate to their new roles. If you have the intent of growth and you act on it through action, you will grow as a startup product manager.

The Power of Tiny Gains by James Clear

1% **better** every day is equivalent to 1.01^{365} = **37.78 times better**

1% **worse** every day is equivalent to 0.99^{365} = **0.03 times worse**

Source: Jamesclear.com

Why Your First 30 Days as a Startup Product Manager Are Pivotal

We will review the top 10 habits that can compound your growth over time to help you become the best startup product manager you can be. These are habits for your first 30 days and beyond. Startup product management is about developing consistent habits. A skilled startup operator is someone who can efficiently maneuver through challenges, solve problems for their customers, lead teams by example, and create value for the business. Great execution comes from habits and intuition, which are built over time.

Compounding progress can have a substantial impact on the rest of your product management career. Focusing on your strengths and adapting to your weaknesses can help you continuously grow as a startup product manager. Setting strong habits in the first 30 days will redefine your career trajectory.

Habit One: How to Become a Product Expert

1. Use The Product:

Use the product as much as you can in your first 30 days. Try to become an expert on the product. Go through the whole end-to-end flow and understand the user journey. You can start to pick up on what works well, what does not work well, and start gaining empathy for your customers. If you can put yourself in the shoes

273

of your customers, that is the first way you can start solving problems — and start building as a startup product manager.

Find bugs in the product and report them. Identifying bugs in the product is one way to gain a deeper understanding of how the product works. This will also help you get early exposure with engineering.

Habit Two: How to Use Precedents to Understand Product Strategy And Execution

2. Read PRDs, User Stories, Documentation, and Roadmap:

Study the precedents that have been set. Learn how PRDs have been written. Study how problem statements are crafted and the level of detail you should expect to have in PRDs. Understand the process of your company and learn what your product teams found valuable previously in PRDs.

Read user stories. If your role involves writing user stories, you should understand how they are written at your company. You can also learn about how to write great user stories that empower your teams as seen in a previous chapter.

Reading documentation. Documentation will help provide context and understand how the product was meant to be used. They should be supplemental resources to assist in your learning of the product.

Study the roadmap. Align on the product vision. If a roadmap exists, you can learn more about the roadmap. Even if it does not exist, you can play a role in defining it later. I would recommend setting up a meeting with your founder, your head of product, or anyone who had a role in creating the roadmap if it exists. They can provide their perspectives on the product strategy. They can explain and talk about it in ways that will provide unique context and clarity into the vision of the product. If you can understand and start to address the top priorities of the company, you will often get tasked to solve challenging problems and be trusted with more responsibility.

Habit Three: How to Build Stakeholder Relationships Early On

3. Meet With Your Stakeholders:

Learn about their goals. Ask them about their top goals, how you can help improve the team, and how you can drive better alignment.

Learn about who they are and find common ground. Each person has a unique story. What do they enjoy the most about what they do? Why do they enjoy it? What is their background? Do they have hobbies and interests? Try to find common ground.

Do not focus on process changes on day one. It is important to listen first. Listen to your stakeholders first because it takes time to get the context to make the decision. Once you have alignment on values and goals, it is much easier to drive change. It is never too early to make changes, but successful change requires trust. Change is often driven by collaboration and alignment. Team buy-in and empowerment drives lasting change and impactful problem solving.

Understand the specific goals of your designers, engineers, and business teams.

- When talking to **designers**, you should talk about what an ideal partnership would be between product and design. How do they prefer to have design critiques?
- When talking to **engineers**, you should talk to them about what an ideal partnership would be between product and engineering. What would they like to see more of in PRDs? If you are writing tickets, what would they like to see?
- When talking to **sales** and **marketing**, you should ask them about what they are seeing with potential prospects. In your first 30 to 60 days, you should understand the patterns these teams are seeing with customers and find the common threads. Does marketing track funnel analytics? What are interesting findings they have had?
- When talking to **customer success**, you should ask them about their recent interactions with customers, insights about current and past customers, and how customers use the product. How do they define success? Are there any

blockers for them? How can product and customer success work effectively to solve important problems and have a clear communication channel?

Habit Four: How to Deliver a Large Impact From Day One

4. Ship Something:

Learn what it takes to solve a problem and find a solution at your company. Product Management is about solving the right problem and facilitating the right solution. You may or may not be given a problem to solve in your first 30 days. Find a problem to solve — by looking at your data, talking to customers, and helping your team in any way. The solution can be one small feature, one large feature, or multiple features. Try shipping something. Learn about what it takes to ship a feature and how it works at your company.

Habit Five: How to Become a Market Expert For Your Product

5. Become Familiar With The Industry:

You will need to know how your company will uniquely position itself to disrupt the industry it operates in. You need to know how your product can provide value to your customers and get an idea of how the product will scale. What is your company's strategy and plan for execution within the context of the broader industry? Understand the industry your company operates in. This helps you contextualize your product team's strategy in a broader scope. It will help you be more informed when making key decisions in your next month, year, and beyond as a startup product manager.

There are some ways you can do this:

- **Ask questions**: you have to do the initial, upfront research. You can achieve this by using the product, understand why it adds value, and *then* anticipate the future vision of the product. You can form deep questions to ask your team. Bring value to them by showing that you have thoughtfully segmented the personas for your product, what their greatest challenges are, how the current product solves your customers' problems, and how your product can solve your customers' problems in the future. Ask your manager and your founder(s) how they currently envision the product as well as the future state. Align with their understanding of the product vision, strategy, business model, and go-to-market strategy. Learn from them **why** the product is being built this way, **how** your company is prioritizing changes, and **how** you will sell & scale the product.
- **Learn why your investors invested in your company:** read the press releases online, the investor memos, your

investors' social media posts on the company, their public appearances talking about the industry or your company, and investigate any data from Crunchbase or Pitchbook. Reach out to VCs or read content from VCs to gain context into the space.

- **Conduct your own market research: read internal resources and contextualize them with what you read online.** Learn how your company's strategy makes sense, compare your company to your core competitors, discover the trends in the industry, and beyond. Are you <u>vertically integrating</u> a solution? Is it a highly fragmented industry that you are operating in? Is it very competitive? Is there consolidation happening? Especially at early stage startups, you will need to teach yourself a lot and ask questions to the experts. You may have an onboarding program that covers this, but you can always do this on your own too. Find the facts and do your own research. Learn a bit about the ins and outs of your product, watch YouTube videos, listen to podcasts, and more. You can also go to industry events, either online or in-person.

Habit Six: How to Use Data to
Tell Stories And Identify Opportunities

6. Become Familiar With Your Product Analytics:

Before talking to customers, you can look at your product analytics. If you are at a larger tech company right now, you likely have analytics in place. All startups should have tracking and analytics in place. It holds you and various stakeholders accountable for decisions that are made. When you have product analytics and tracking in place, you can thoughtfully track the impact of your decisions and go beyond gut-feeling. In order to become great at prioritization and execution, you need to have a mastery over your data as a startup product manager. Analytics are absolutely crucial to your role as a startup product manager. Also, if you are at an early-stage startup: this can be a critical asset to your long-term growth as a company. You can use them to validate or invalidate hypotheses and run experiments to promote the growth of your product.

You do not need to become analytics-obsessed, but learn how to use it to supplement *how* you are solving problems for your customers. Remember to look at the long-term value for customers. Understand what will bring value a year or a decade from now. While quick wins are important, you will not win by solely optimizing short-term value for your customers. You also need to make long-term investments and build features that may not have an immediate impact on your data but will deliver long-term value for your customers.

You need to be able to quantify the qualitative behavior of your customers. Can you watch recordings of how customers use the product? Can you analyze the end to end flow of the customer? Can you see where they are converting, where they are not converting? This will paint pictures and tell you stories, as well as help you see pain points your customers are experiencing. You will understand where the user experience can be improved, through learning more about where they struggle to complete a flow and where they face problems with your product. You will also be able to pinpoint problems that customers may not have been explicitly articulated or communicated.

Habit Seven: How to Understand Your Customers Quickly And Deeply

7. Start understanding WHO your customers are:

Understand who is using your product and who you are providing value to. Are there personas that the team has created? Can you think of the ideal persona? Ask your manager, designers, marketers, or other team members who the typical customers are. You can also start talking to customers to gain a perspective into the different personas, the problems they each experience, their likes and dislikes, and how your team is designing solutions for them.

Habit Eight: How to Creatively Accelerate Your Learning

8. Follow product managers and join communities:

I recommend following product managers, finding mentors, and interacting with peers. See the previous chapter on the top product managers you can learn from right now.

You could comment on Twitter posts, go to meetups and events, join Slack communities, and meet others. It is important to get yourself out there and meet people who are in your shoes (or were once in your shoes). You can begin to find those who are building products at startups and larger tech companies. It can be fun to find your community and meet others, either in-person or virtually.

Habit Nine: How to Focus and Drive Impactful Outcomes

9. Focus on the fundamentals:

Remember to keep it simple and focus on the fundamentals. In order to effectively solve problems on the job, you need to keep it simple. Most answers and solutions to your problems are right in front of you. The most effective ways to brainstorm ideas is through your conversations with customers, your collaboration with your teammates, your abilities to bring people together, your experiences using the product, and your time at the company. This is the most important advice I would give: focus on the basics. Learn to change up your strategy and experiment as well.

Habit Ten: How to Work on The Most Important Problems

10. Prioritize:

Learn to prioritize. Prioritization is a skill you can grow over time and keep getting better at. The skillset of focusing and executing on the right opportunities at the right time is the key to startup product management. If you want to set yourself apart, you need to learn great execution first. Prioritization is the skill that will enable you to work on the most important problems and drive impactful change for your startup. It is also a skill that you can take with you throughout the rest of your career and life. Prioritization is progress. Focus, discipline, and adaptability will set you apart as a startup product manager. See the previous chapter on how to prioritize effectively as a startup product manager.

CHAPTER 19

MY TOP LESSONS FROM STARTUP PRODUCT MANAGEMENT: THE PRODUCT MENTALITY

In this final chapter, you will discover "the product mentality" and have a chance to absorb my most important learnings and lessons from startup product management. From the many ups and downs of building various startups, I want to share the most helpful and tactical strategies that will benefit you as a startup product manager in the future. This chapter will also solidify your own beliefs in growing as a startup product manager or becoming one in the future. If you have come this far, you need to know that this chapter is one that cannot be missed. The product mentality is a series of ten lessons I have learned from working in product management at startups so far.

Why Startup Product Managers Can Anticipate And Solve Diverse Problems

1. As a product manager, you learn to solve a diverse set of problems. You learn to anticipate problems and discover opportunities to become a better problem solver.

When you become a startup product manager, you develop a mindset of generalist thinking. You are exposed to several different types of problems on a weekly basis, and your brain adapts better to various situations over time. You gain an ability to determine a path to solving almost any problem that you can identify. Startup product managers either solve problems themselves or enlist the help of their team members. You develop skills for solving scavenger hunts efficiently, identifying patterns by thinking connectively, and learning to solve problems efficiently. This ability will be something you continue to grow over your career.

As a startup product manager, you will find that your ability to find and solve problems compounds over time. You will understand how to prioritize and navigate challenges more effectively. You will anticipate how to improve. Startup product managers are always thinking about how to become better. These lessons can be applied to anything you pursue after.

Startup product managers are always asking who, what, where, when, and why. Who is the target customer we are solving for? What are their primary pain points? Where can the existing experience be improved or optimized? When do our customers experience these pain points? Why are these problems important for us to solve?

Startup product managers are talking to customers, asking experts, trusting the specialists, conducting competitive analyses, doing market research, thinking about edge cases, and more. These are skills that are core to several other aspects of business and life.

Why Startup Product Managers Become Great Business Builders

2. At a startup, you are learning how to build a business. Startup product managers hone their founder-mindset everyday. This career path equips you with the holistic skills and confidence to start anything you want to one day.

There are a few basics to product management: understanding what is important for your customers and your business, knowing how to communicate, and learning how to prioritize.

My advice would be to learn as much as you can from others. It is simple: absorb as much information as you can, from those who have done what you want to do. Learn from those who have experience. The important part of this is that you should pick and choose what works well for **you** and your company. There are several product frameworks and resources out there. You need to prioritize what you learn from others and apply what works. If it does not work, do not use it. If it does work, use it. Move fast and iterate.

Having a growth mindset is one of the most important skills a product manager can have. I believe that individuals can develop tactical skills over time and become great product managers. No one has exceptional product talents from the get-go. Yes, some people are more interested in products and building from an early age. I used to review iPhone apps and have different side hustles as a kid. These "talents" were not innate: they were skills I had an interest in developing over time. Yes, you can have interests and inspirations. These need to be crafted through hard work and discipline. You can become anyone who you want to be, with the right amount of effort and focus. Product managers need to believe that they can become anyone who they want to become and should view themselves as highly as they can. Certain product managers have an inclination for certain skills, but they also work **very very** hard at developing them. Pursue your curiosity, and pursue it relentlessly.

Anyone can grow into becoming a Startup Product Manager. These are a few of the many skills that are important that you can build and grow:

- Product "sense" is knowing how to anticipate a great solution for a problem. It also involves being able to detect problems that customers have even if they do not explicitly talk about them. Product sense involves forming a well-grounded hypothesis, creating a solution, and investing time into making a good user experience.

- Product "execution" is about turning an idea into reality. It is about mobilizing individuals around the solution and giving them the necessary context to solve the problem.

- Product "design" is about understanding and empathizing with people and creating solutions. You become great at understanding user experience and visual design by designing, as well as by studying human behavior. You can learn from great designers and those who were in your shoes previously. You can study human psychology, read academic studies, review design principles, and more. You also become better at design by using more products, critiquing products, and redesigning them.

- Identifying a "north star" is having a clear goal for the business and your team. Everyone needs to be aligned on common goals for the startup. When people know what they are working towards, they will figure out how to get there. It also helps keep your team motivated and focused because they now have a clear target to aim for.

Why Startup Product Managers Become Efficient Learners

3. You become a more efficient operator and learner as a startup product manager, as you gain more experience. You learn how to learn quickly as a product manager at a startup.

Product management is difficult in the beginning, especially in your first role at a startup. You are learning the fundamentals of the job while still understanding how to have an impact. Luckily, as you gain more experience, you will be able to anticipate the curveballs and challenges better. You will be responsible for greater scope and tasked to identify, as well as solve, more challenging problems over time.

Given the speed and pace of startups, the difference between a new and experienced product manager is often how disciplined you are in approaching an opportunity. You need to critically think about what problems exist, whether problems are worth solving, and which problems to solve for your customers. And you cannot solve **every** problem at once. The discipline comes in understanding the right problem(s) to solve for your business at that time. There needs to be short-term and long-term hypotheses that you test. For instance, you may ship several small features and improvements on an existing product: these are short-term changes that can optimize the product. On the other hand, you may think about new business opportunities to enter an entirely new market or take on a unique business risk: these are long-term opportunities that can differentiate the product and solve challenging problems. You need to consistently evaluate your strategy as a product manager at a startup. The ability to balance short-term bets and long-term bets is a skill that you can develop over time.

Also, throughout your career as a product manager, you may work for different types of businesses: B2B, B2C, or B2B2C. Learning how to build products within different business models will challenge you to grow as a startup product manager if you have a chance to explore them.

Why Startup Product Managers Become Effective Business Leaders and Acquire Great Leadership Values

4. You learn how to become an effective business leader at a startup and acquire great leadership values.

Being a startup product manager gives you exposure to senior leadership, and this can be especially helpful very early on in your career. You may work with the CEO, other co-founders, the head of customer success, head of design, head of marketing, head of engineering, head of sales, and more.

Through this exposure, you start to identify signals of great leadership for a business as a whole as well as specific signals for each functional niche. As you continue to work at multiple startups and interface with more senior leaders over time, you begin to develop an intuition for identifying great leaders. You also begin to develop a sense for differentiating leaders who make an impact and know what they are talking about, versus leaders who do not make an impact and may not know what they are talking about. Startup product managers have the unique opportunity to interface with most leaders across different functional groups. When you get to work at startups, you get to see both sides of the spectrum: good and bad leadership. The best way to become a leader is to see all forms of leadership and learn from it. This can be also helpful as you continue in your career to find more product management opportunities at startups, hire for your own company one day, or invest in startups in the future.

In terms of what you could look for in a leader, you may look for someone who fosters a culture of openness, experimentation, alignment, mutual respect, diversity of opinions and backgrounds, a clear focus, and a long term vision. Trust and integrity are paramount as well. Leaders help their team members feel secure and empower them to do their best work.

As a startup product manager, you will gain a lot of exposure into what each leader in an organization works on from a functional standpoint. You get to learn about what they focus on day to day and what they find valuable. Product management is a bridge to different organizations at a startup, and you will develop a sense for how to work with each function as well as how to understand what effective leaders do in each functional team.

Product management is about people. You need to learn to communicate, trust, empower, and delegate to other teams. The interpersonal skills of product management are especially important if you hope to run a business one day. Time is limited as a product manager or founder. You will need to work with others and find innovative ways to delegate. Product managers need to focus on deciding what to build and executing on it. The more they can work with others, the more fluidly a startup will run.

Why Startup Product Management Opens Doors for Your Career

5. Startups are a long-term game you can play in throughout your career. Being a product manager at a startup opens doors for you.

Working as a startup product manager can give you the foundation to be involved in the startup world for the rest of your career. You understand what it takes to build a startup, both from failure and success. These lessons add to your existing knowledge base over time. After being a product manager at a startup once, you can continue to build other startups as a product manager and become better over time.

The other benefit of being a product manager at a startup is being part of a community of other early stage builders. You can network with other product managers as well as mentor up-and-coming product managers. There are experienced product managers who also advise founders and invest in startups as well. Early stage product managers often also go on becoming founders of their own businesses or joining the venture world full-time as investors in other startups.

The Art of Startup Product Management is Qualitative and Quantitative

6. The art of problem solving in product management is quantitative and qualitative. It is important to have a balance.

Product management is quantitative in that you need to use **data** to validate or invalidate the hypotheses you have. It is also easier to influence without authority when you have access to data. You can add depth to opinions or thoughts by incorporating data. As a startup product manager, you need to be knowledgeable about data. Tracking metrics can quantify customer behavior and help you make sense of your customers at scale. Data helps you understand the opportunity areas for the business, and when you launch features, it can help you evaluate how your features perform. Data is also important because it helps prove or disprove any beliefs that you or another team member has. Often, within certain bounds, there is no right or wrong idea until you test and measure the results. You can always test a hypothesis and then see what is right. Teams that use data are more informed when making decisions and also open to experimentation. Startup product management is about moving fast, trying new things, and measuring the impact of those changes.

Product management is qualitative in that you need to **talk** to people: you need to talk to customers, you need to talk to sales and customer success, you need to work with various stakeholders to build products, and more. Startup product managers have to gather data through asking questions to customers and stakeholders. They also play a major role in communicating how they solve problems collaboratively across different teams. Stakeholder communication is a large part of the role, and in order to make progress on product decisions, it often requires interaction with various stakeholders to gather their input or get their help when executing on opportunities.

Startup product management requires a balance between the quantitative and qualitative aspects of the role in order to build innovative products that solve problems for your customers.

Startup Product Managers Learn to Advocate for Themselves

7. You get to learn how to advocate for yourself internally and externally.

When you and your team are doing great work, you should commend those involved in a project and communicate it to your broader team. Learning to manage up is important. You need to keep your manager and any relevant stakeholders informed about what you work on and what your team works on. Startup product managers need to consistently highlight the impact of their releases. Otherwise, no one will know because everyone is busy working on their own initiatives. At a startup, you need to find time to communicate up to executives and across different teams.

This is often hard to do because you are so focused on execution: making sure you are solving problems, releasing features, and delivering an impact. The difficult part is reminding yourself to **communicate** the *outcome* of what you work on, as well as what you are working on.

As a startup product manager, your initial goals involve improving the business and helping customers. If you are delivering positive outcomes, you need to advocate for yourself as well. You need to optimize for what is best for you, whether it is skill development, your career trajectory, the types of opportunities, or anything else. Usually, if you follow through on what you work on and add value to the business, you can typically build opportunities for yourself to optimize for your career. The more value you provide to the business and when people know about it, the more you can open doors for yourself as a startup product manager.

Also, you need to advocate for yourself externally. Start documenting your learnings on product management. The field of startup product management is still new. It is important that you think deeply about how you can build your career journey outside of work as well. Whether it is through hobbies and passions you may have, you should document what you do. It is an easy way to create your brand. You can write, talk, or build. Think of your career as a video game, and you are the main character. Continue to build your character, develop new skills, and seek out experiences. Specifically, it is valuable for you to build your brand externally because you can discover new opportunities to grow in your career beyond your current role. My motivation to build my brand involves continuing to help individuals get into the field of product management, helping people join startups, and helping me get closer to my personal goals long-term. You need to be intentional about advocating for yourself externally. It allows you to further your own career as well as the careers of others. You can increase your impact on the world around you through building your brand.

Startup Product Managers Learn Everything About Product Management

8. You get to explore different forms of product management at a startup.

At a startup, you are likely going to be a generalist product manager if a startup is relatively new or even if you are early in your career. This means that you will learn a little bit of everything. Startup product managers are end-to-end generalists, which trains them to become business builders. Typically, in your startup career, you will start out as a generalist. Startup product managers get to work on the core product, interact with nearly every team, launch experiments, work on growth initiatives, build out API integrations, learn across different business models (B2B, B2C, B2B2C), and more. You get to delve into many different skills at a startup.

As a generalist, after working in different product management roles at a startup, you eventually start to become more self-aware of the skills and the work that interests you. Start to understand what type of work fuels you. The best part of working at a startup is that you get to sample different forms of product management. There are certain forms of product management you will gravitate towards and invest more time into learning. As you grow in your career and gain more expertise, you can pick and choose the types of product management work you enjoy.

Why Startup Product Managers Make High-Impact Decisions

9. You learn how to focus and make high-impact decisions.

Startup product managers have to work on opportunities that move the needle for the business and its customers. Early stage businesses run lean and have limited resources, and there is pressure to scale quickly. Naturally, the initiatives you work on will have to be impactful for the business and its customers. You are helping your customers find a solution that is better than what exists out on the market and making an impact in their lives. A startup optimizes for growth or profitability. If the startup has found product-market fit and has potential of profitability, it can have 1) low growth and higher likelihood of profitability or 2) high growth and lower likelihood profitability. The important part is that growth and profitability are the two most important cornerstones of scaling a business. Startup product managers are in charge of building the best business possible and constantly improving the user experience of the product they are building.

Startup product managers have to learn to zoom in and zoom out. Day to day, you will focus on execution and working with various teams to help ideas become a reality. You also have to learn how to focus on the bigger picture. Startup product managers need to consciously evaluate if what they are doing is driving the business forward, as well as what opportunities they can take on that can help the business in new ways.

Startup product managers cannot conflate activity with progress. "Activity" involves execution and doing what is expected of you as a product manager to deliver a feature. "Progress" involves solving hard problems, working on high impact opportunities, and asking yourself the tough questions. Startup product managers need to ask themselves the following questions: what will create a noticeable impact for my business and for my customers? How am I prioritizing the most important initiatives today, this week, and beyond? It is important to differentiate a high-impact decision and a high-impact feature. Not every feature you build or deliver will have a high impact. As mentioned before, there are short-term and long-term features that you will have to build. However, you have to make the right decisions for your business and customers. Every decision a startup product manager makes has a high downstream impact: it influences what your design teams work on, what your engineering teams build, what your marketing teams run ads on and create content for, what your sales teams pitch to potential prospects, and more.

Your time as a product manager is split into making decisions, executing on a strategy, and defining the future strategy. It is particularly important to reflect on what you are working on over a period of time. You should think about what you prioritize for the day, a week, a month, a quarter. This involves also saying "no" when it does not fit into your priorities. It starts out with thinking small and shifting your thinking to the higher level strategy of what is important.

Resilience: Do Work That Excites You – And Do Work That Does Not

10. Do work that excites you — in an industry or at a company that motivates you. But remember that you have to often do work you do not initially want to do, and you will be better off as a product manager for doing so.

Your career goals may involve exploring your curiosity. It is intuitive to work on things that **you** want to work on, so it makes sense that you should actively pursue what you are interested in. This may be about joining a vision that you care about or even joining an industry that aligns with where you want to be. For example, if you want to work in FinTech, you can work at a company that builds these types of products. If you want to work for a mission-driven company, you should actively filter for those companies and be open to those opportunities. The reason I say this is that you can find individuals with like-minded goals who have shared values and a shared mission. Within these opportunities, you will also find people who are very different from you as well. In your startup product management career, it can help that you identify a culture and build a foundation that fits your personality & goals. It helps to know why you are doing what you are doing, as well as find a culture that fits that "why."

However, the caveat here is that part of the job is doing things you do not want to do. Startup product management has work that is fun and not fun. On the job, startup product managers have to be scrappy and wear multiple hats. You may enjoy certain types of work and may not want to do certain types of work. At any job, you will have a mix of projects that will vary in terms of your personal interests. You need to learn how to build through discipline. You may not be motivated to work on everything. But that is when you grow the most and become a true product manager. Startup product managers often go on to become founders. Founders do not get to work on the most exciting problems every single minute of their day. There are a lot of parts of the job that are not exciting. The most important lesson of product management at startups for me has been building resilience. Resilience is something you can continue to grow over time, and you can continue to bring it with you throughout the rest of your career. Building resilience has been one of the greatest parts of the journey of startup product management. I hope that one day you have the opportunity to navigate the ups and downs of the startup journey as a product manager.

There are a lot of tactical lessons that were shared throughout this book, but the most important lesson I can share is to continue to be resilient in the way you see yourself. Visualize yourself in the highest way possible and execute on that vision you have for yourself. The mindset you have will help you throughout your career, and hopefully one day too, you can pay it forward to the next generation of startup builders. I am excited to see the startup product leaders who will build the future small and medium businesses of the world. I hope this book can continue to be a guide for you in your journey. You *will* become a great startup product manager.

Made in United States
North Haven, CT
08 August 2023

40090679R00170